Dictionary of Medical Astrology

A Compilation of Astrological Terms
(Physical, Emotional and Mental)
and Disease Significators
Used in Traditional Medical Astrology

Diane L. Cramer, MS, CA NCGR

ISBN-10: 0-86690-539-1
ISBN-13: 978-0-86690-539-8

Cover Design: Jack Cipolla

Published by:
American Federation of Astrologers, Inc.
6535 S. Rural Road
Tempe AZ 85283

Printed in the United States of America

Acknowledgements

The author wishes to acknowledge
Ronnie Cramer, Karen Christino, Bob Marks,
Barbara Kaminsky, Angela Petrocelli,
Catherine Thomas and Liane Thomas Wade
for their assistance and support.

Contents

Introduction

How to Use this Dictionary

The dictionary that follows contains the most commonly agreed-upon meanings of terms used in medical astrology. In utilizing the works of other medical astrologers to compile this dictionary one is faced with a lack of agreement as to what rules what in the body. One source will cite a planet for a particular organ, another source will cite a sign for the same organ and another source will cite a completely different sign or planet for the same organ. In some cases there are several meanings for the same part of the body, which only adds to the confusion. Since some organs are involved in more than one bodily process, they can be ruled by more than one sign or planet, depending on which of its functions is being described. With the disagreement among medical astrologers as to what rules what, it is necessary to establish a criteria on which to base the meanings of the medical terms used in medical astrology. When several meanings were given for the same term or when there was no meaning given for a particular term, the author used the criteria that follows to determine rulership.

The easiest way to determine whether a planet or sign rules a particular disease or part of the body is to assume that the signs of the zodiac refer to the anatomical locations in the body, i.e., Aries is the head, Pisces is the feet and that the planets refer to physiological action. Mars in Cancer thus increases stomach acid, whereas Saturn in Cancer indicates a decrease of acid in the stomach. This is medical astrology in its simplest form. However, one will find that sometimes a sign, like a planet, rules a bodily process. One must have an understanding of the physiological action of each planet in medical astrology and the effects of the planets on the signs to understand why a particular combination rules a bodily action or location. And an understanding of the action of the signs as well as their anatomical location in the body will help the reader to understand the definitions that follow. It will also become clearer why a particular combination rules a specific disease state.

The following is a brief description of the nature and actions of the signs and planets in medical astrology. An understanding of their action will help the reader to understand the various rulershps that follow in the dictionary.

(For a fuller explanation of the signs and planets in medical astrology, see *How to Give an Astrological Health Reading*.)

Signs in Relation to Illness

Aries, which is fiery, hot and dry, is descriptive of heat, inflammation and energy.

Taurus, which is earthy, cold and dry, is a sign that aggregates and assembles. It can aid in the support and endurance of the body.

Gemini, which is airy, hot and moist, is involved in linkages and transference and can be descriptive of restlessness and nervousness. It is a connector and rules the tubes of the body.

Cancer, which is watery, moist and cold, rules all coverings and containers in the body. It encloses, protects and nurtures.

Leo, which is fiery, hot and dry, is a sign of energy and vitality. It can be vivifying.

Virgo, which is earthy, cold and dry, rules the processes of assimilation, selection and utilization in the body. It rules the process of discrimination and is involved in splitting and separating and analyzing.

Libra, which is airy, hot and moist, refers to the principle of balance and the processes of filtration and distillation. Libra evaluates and adjusts.

Scorpio, which is cold and watery, rules elimination, ejection and destruction. It has the ability to throw off and readapt itself.

Sagittarius, which is fiery, hot and dry, can refer to locomotion and transference. It aims and projects.

Capricorn, which is earthy, cold and dry, refers to limitation and the processes of hardening and inhibition. It controls and manages.

Aquarius, which is airy, hot and moist, rules cooperation, associational processes, and differentness.

Pisces, which is watery, cold and moist, can have a relaxing and softening effect. It breaks down barriers and is a sign of universality.

Of great importance are the polarities between signs. An affliction in Aries can indicate a medical problem in a Libra ruled organ or tissue, and vice versa. And going a step further, an affliction in any one or more signs of a quadruplicity can indicate a medical problem in any one of the four signs of the quadruplicity. Hence, an affliction in Taurus could manifest in a Taurus-related organ or in an organ ruled by Scorpio, Leo or Aquarius.

Planets in Relation to Illness

The Sun is indicative of inflammation, infection, fever and energy problems.

The Moon rules inconstancy, emotional disorders, water balance and bodily cycles.

Mercury is involved with the respiratory and nervous system. It describes one's mental health.

Venus rules sugar, venous circulation, balance and cosmetic skin problems.

Mars rules infection and inflammation and acute disorders. It rules acidity, surgery, accidents, irritation, the muscles and blood ailments.

Jupiter enlarges and rules arterial blood circulation, fat assimilation and the function of the liver.

Saturn, which is alkaline, constricts, limits, hardens and obstructs. It rules chronic disease and underactivity.

Uranus, which can be explosive, rules incoordination, spasm, accidents, surgery, electricity and seizures.

Neptune softens and relaxes and rules drugs, alcohol, poisons, misdiagnosis, the immune system, and malignancy.

Pluto can also refer to malignancy and rules malformation, hereditary disorders, massive infection, bodily transformation and amputation.

This brief introduction to rulerships in medical astrology is given to help the reader to understand the rulerships and astrological signatures of diseases and medical terminology that follows.

As stated previously, the dictionary that follows uses the most commonly agreed-upon medical astrology definitions. When more than one planet is listed, it is assumed that the planets are in stress aspect with each other or in a midpoint combination. There are times, however, when just having a particular planetary combination indicates a specific disorder in the body. Thus, occasionally, planets in harmonious aspect can point to a particular disease if the planets involved are not sympathetic to each other.

When more than one definition was found, it was also listed, but in all cases the most common definition is listed first. At times it might not be obvious to the reader why a particular signature is listed. This is because sometimes one is seeing the rulership of the underlying cause of a disease or bodily function, and at other times one is seeing the actual location of the disease.

The rulership of vitamins and minerals can be purely arbitrary. Vitamins and minerals are involved in many bodily processes and probably cannot be simplified as to one rulership but should be ruled according to the function described. One rarely finds agreement on these rulerships among medical astrologers, and those chosen for the dictionary describe one or more of the primary functions of the vitamin or mineral listed. This is also true of the endocrine system and the various glands in the body.

It goes without saying that the more one knows about medical astrology and the body, the better one will have an understanding of the terms used. One must be a proficient astrologer first to understand medical astrology. Then one must get used to using a medical dictionary, an anatomy book and books such as the *Merck Manual of Medical Information* to hone one's skills.

This dictionary is geared to the layperson who has a limited knowledge of medicine. It does not purport to be complete but does include what the author feels were the most common diseases and/or terms used in medical astrology. This is not the final word on rulership in medical astrology, but more a beginning. The reader is directed to the Bibliography for more information.

Diane L. Cramer
July 2013

A

Abdomen: Cancer

Abdominal cavity: Cancer

Abdominal distention: Jupiter Neptune

Abdominal problems: Mars or Saturn in Cancer

Abnormal growth: Jupiter Pluto

Abnormal persons: Neptune

Abnormality: Pluto, Uranus

Abortion: Mars in Scorpio, Moon Uranus, Moon Mars

Abortion, spontaneous: fifth house, Uranus

Abrasions: Mars

Abscesses: Pluto, Venus afflicted, Taurus, Mars Neptune or Mars Pluto afflictions

Absorbent: Moon

Absorption: Virgo, Mercury

Accident prone: Mars Ascendant, Sun, Moon or Ascendant in combination with Mars Uranus

Accidents: Sun Mars, Moon Mars, Mars Uranus, Mars Ascendant

Accidents, electrical: Uranus Pluto

Accidents from gas: Mars Neptune

Accidents from horses: Sagittarius, Mars in Sagittarius

Accidents from machinery: Mars Uranus, Uranus Pluto

Accidents in the home: Moon Mars

1

Aches: Saturn

Achondroplasia: Capricorn

Acid: Mars

Acid alkaline imbalance: Aries Libra, Venus Mars, Venus Saturn

Acid base balance: Libra

Acidosis: Mars, Sun Mars affliction, Mars in cardinal sign, Mercury Mars

Acid stomach: Moon Mars, Mars in Cancer

Acne: Venus stress aspect, Venus Uranus, Venus Pluto, Aries, Mars in Aries, first house

Acoustic neuroma: Saturn in Aries

Acromegaly: Aries, Jupiter in Aries, Jupiter in Gemini, Jupiter in Pisces

Acromicria: Capricorn, Saturn in Aries, Saturn in Gemini

Acupuncture: Mars Neptune

Acute: Mars

Acute disease: Cardinality, Mutability, Mars

Adaptation: Moon

ADD (Attention Deficit Disorder): Mercury Mars, Mercury Uranus, Saturn Uranus, Sun or Moon Uranus, Mercury retrograde

Addiction: Neptune Ascendant, Moon Neptune, Jupiter Neptune, Mars Neptune, Moon = Mars/Neptune

Addison's Disease: Mars Saturn, Saturn in Aries

Adenoids: Taurus Scorpio

Adenoids, enlargement: Jupiter in Taurus, afflictions in Libra or Scorpio or their rulers along with afflictions in Aries

Adhesions: Saturn

Adhesive: Saturn

Adipose tissue: Jupiter

Adoption: Neptune in fifth house, Neptune in fourth house

Adrenal action: Mars

Adrenal medulla: Aries, Mars

Adrenaline: Mars

Adrenal insufficiency: Mars Neptune, Mars Saturn

Aggregation: Taurus

Aging process: Saturn

Agitation: Moon Uranus, Moon Mars, Uranus

Aggression, over: Mars Saturn, Mars Pluto, Saturn Pluto, Mars Uranus

AIDS: mutability, Mars Neptune; Mars Pluto, eighth house emphasis, prominent Neptune, low earth, Venus Retrograde, Moon Saturn or Saturn Neptune combinations, Neptune rising ahead of the Sun, Mars/Neptune = Sun, Ascendant or Pluto, Saturn = Venus/Mars, Jupiter = Neptune/Pluto

AIDS survival: emphasis in Scorpio, Sagittarius, Aquarius, **Jupiter or Uranus = Mars/Saturn, water emphasis**

Albumin: Cancer

Alcohol: Neptune

Alcoholism: Mars in Pisces, Angular Neptune, Sun Neptune, Moon Neptune, Moon Mars, Mars Neptune, Mars square Uranus, Weak Sun or Moon in fire or water, twelfth house emphasis, Sun, Moon or Mercury to Neptune, Moon, Jupiter or Mars to Uranus

Alimentary canal: Taurus Cancer Virgo Scorpio

Alkalinity: Saturn, Sun Saturn

Alkaloids: Neptune

Allergies: prominent Moon or Neptune, Moon stress Neptune, Pluto in sixth house, Sun Neptune, water signs, see also Respiratory Allergies

Allergies to cosmetics: Venus in Aries

Alopecia: Aries, Fire emphasis

Alopecia pimples: Aries

Alzheimer's: Uranus, Saturn, Neptune aspecting Sun or Moon, Aries emphasis, Aquarius emphasis, Mercury Neptune

Aluminum: Uranus

Ambidexterity: Mercury in Pisces, Jupiter in Gemini, Mercury Neptune, Mercury Mars

Amenorrhea: Saturn in Scorpio, Moon Saturn, Venus Saturn

Amino acid formation: Virgo

Amino acids: Mars

Amnesia: Moon Mercury in stress aspect, Neptune

Amniotic fluid: Moon, Cancer

Amputation: Mars Pluto, Saturn Uranus, Saturn Ascendant, Pluto

Anabolic processes: Venus Jupiter, Sun Mars

Analgesia: Neptune

Anemia: Sun Neptune, Saturn in Cancer, Saturn in Aquarius, Sun stress aspect to Uranus in Libra or Aquarius, Moon Mars Pluto combination, Neptune and Saturn in stress to Mars.

Anemia, microcytic: Moon Mars, Mars Jupiter, Mars Saturn, Mars Neptune, Saturn Pluto affliction and sign of Cancer involved:

Anemia, pernicious: Saturn in Cancer, Sun Neptune, Sun Saturn, Pluto = Sun/Neptune, Neptune = Sun/Pluto, Sun = Neptune/Pluto

Anesthesia: Neptune

Anesthetics: Neptune

Aneurysm: Saturn, Aries, Leo

Anger: Mars Uranus

Angina: Mars in Leo

Anguish: eighth house

Ankles: Aquarius

Ankylosis: Saturn in Capricorn, Sun Mars

4

Ankylosing spondylitis: Saturn, Saturn in Leo, Leo Aquarius

Anorexia: Saturn in Cancer or Capricorn, Saturn in fourth or tenth house, Moon in Aquarius

Anterior pituitary gland: Capricorn, Saturn, Scorpio

Anthrax: Saturn Neptune, Neptune

Antibiotics: Pluto, sixth house

Antibody: Neptune

Antigen: Neptune

Antihistamine: Neptune

Antiphlogistic: Saturn

Antipyretic: Saturn

Antiseptic: Neptune

Antispasmodic: Mars Saturn Uranus

Anuria: Saturn in Libra, Saturn in Scorpio

Anus: Scorpio

Anxiety: Saturn Neptune, Moon Neptune, Moon Saturn, Sun Uranus, Gemini, Saturn = Pluto/Ascendant

Aorta: Leo

Apathy: Saturn

Aphasia: Pluto, Mercury, Saturn in Aries, Mercury Saturn

Apnea: Saturn in Aquarius, Saturn in Gemini

Apothecary: Mars, Scorpio, Mercury

Apoplexy: Aries, Sun Jupiter

Appendicitis: Mars in Virgo, Saturn in Virgo, Virgo and Scorpio afflictions, Uranus in stress aspect, Mercury in stress aspect to a malefic, Neptune = Venus/Mars

Appendix vermiform: Virgo, Scorpio, Pisces

Appetite: Venus, Jupiter, second house, fourth house

Appetite, poor: Neptune = Sun/Pluto

Apprehension: Moon Neptune

Arches: Pisces

Arches, fallen: Mars in Pisces

5

Argumentative: Mars Uranus in Gemini or third house aspecting Mercury

Armpits: Cancer

Arms: Gemini, Mercury, third house

Arms, artificial: Neptune, Neptune in third house

Arrhythmia: Aquarius, See also Cardiac Arrhythmia

Arrogance: Sun

Arsenic: Mars, Pluto

Arterial blood circulation: Jupiter

Arteries, blocked: Jupiter in Leo or Aquarius, or in fifth or eleventh house with hard aspects from Saturn, Jupiter in Capricorn

Arteriosclerosis: Saturn in Capricorn, Jupiter in Capricorn, Jupiter Saturn, Saturn in fifth house, Saturn in Aquarius, Sun Saturn, Jupiter Saturn

Arthritis: Saturn angular or aspecting Sun or Moon, Mars Saturn Neptune combination, Cardinal emphasis, Saturn in Cancer or Capricorn

Arthritis in arms, hands, shoulders: Saturn in Gemini, Sun Saturn, Mars Saturn, Moon Saturn, Neptune = Mars/Saturn

Articulation: Saturn

Artificial limbs: Mars Pluto

Asbestos poisoning: Saturn Neptune, Gemini

Ascendant: Physical body, conductivity or resistance of body

Asphyxia: Saturn in Aquarius

Assimilation: Virgo Pisces. Jupiter Mercury

Asthma: Moon Mercury Gemini Sagittarius combination; afflictions in Gemini, mutable emphasis, Prominent Mercury, Saturn in Gemini or Sagittarius, Neptune stress to Sun or Moon, Mercury Saturn afflictions, angular Moon, emphasis in Cancer, Saturn afflictions to third house, Saturn in third house, Moon in Virgo or Sagittarius, Taurus or Scorpio prominent

Astral body: Neptune

Astringent: Saturn

Asylums: twelfth house

Ataxia: Mars in Gemini, Mars Neptune, Mars Saturn

Atonicness: Neptune

Atrophy: Saturn, Jupiter Neptune

Augmentation: Sagittarius, Jupiter

Aura: Uranus, Neptune

Autism: Moon, Cancer, Neptune, Venus, emphasis in third and twelfth, retrograde planets, Mercury in twelfth, Mercury or Venus Retrograde, Mercury Mars in Aries

Autistic thinking: Mercury

Autointoxication: Mars Saturn prominent, Neptune Pluto prominent

Autonomic nervous system: Sun Nodes, Mercury

Avoidance: mutability

B

Babies: Cancer

Baby, feverish: Moon Mars

Backache: Leo, Aquarius, Sun aspecting Saturn, Uranus or Neptune

Back, lower: Leo

Back problems: Afflictions in fixed signs, Sun Saturn, Saturn in Leo, Saturn Uranus afflicting other planets

Back, upper: Libra

Bacteria: Neptune, Pluto

Bacterial endocarditis: Cancer, Neptune, Aquarius

Bacteriologist: Pluto, Saturn, Neptune, Uranus

Balance: Libra

Baldness: Aries, Fire signs

Barrenness: Saturn, Moon afflicted to Mars, Saturn or Uranus, Virgo emphasis

Barrier: Saturn

Basal metabolism: Libra

B-complex vitamins: Mercury

Bedwetting: Libra or Scorpio emphasis, prominent Uranus

Belching: Cancer

Bell's Palsy: Aries, Uranus

Benign growth: Venus, Jupiter

Bifocal: Saturn in Gemini

Bile: Jupiter, Virgo, Sagittarius

Bilious flatulence: Mercury in Gemini

Binding: Saturn

Biopsy: Mars Pluto

Biotin: Jupiter

Bi-polar disorder: Gemini Sagittarius, Neptune in first house, Saturn in Libra, Mars afflicted

Birth: Venus Uranus, Mars Jupiter, Sun Pluto, fifth house, Leo

Birth conditions: Ascendant

Birth control: eighth house

Birth control pill: Pluto

Birth defect: Pluto, Neptune Ascendant

Birth trauma: Mars in first house, Pluto Ascendant

Bisexuality: Neptune, Mercury Neptune

Blackheads: Venus

Blackout: Moon Neptune

Bladder: Moon and/or Cancer, Scorpio

Bladder, urinary disorders: Scorpio Taurus, afflicted Moon in Aquarius, Mars, Venus or Mercury afflicted in Scorpio, afflictions in Scorpio or severe afflictions involving Mars or Pluto

Bladder disease: Moon Saturn

Bladder infection: Moon Saturn, Moon Neptune, Moon Pluto, Scorpio

Bladder pain: Moon Saturn, Libra Scorpio, Moon, Venus, Mars

Bladder trouble: Scorpio afflictions, Mars Pluto stress

Bleeding: Saturn Neptune afflictions, Mars or Saturn afflicted

Blemishes: afflictions to Ascendant, Mars Saturn with Libra

Blindness: 29° Taurus, Moon Mars stress aspect, Aries, Mars = Sun/Moon, see also Sight

Blister: Mars, Venus Mars

Bloating: Moon in Cancer

Blood: Mars, Jupiter , Sagittarius, Leo Aquarius

Blood circulation: Aquarius, Sun

Blood clots: Saturn, Earth emphasis

Blood disease: Sun Neptune, Moon Pluto, Venus, Jupiter, Saturn = Sun/Neptune

Blood disease, inherited: Sun/Neptune = Node

Blood disorders: Jupiter afflicted, Mars Saturn, Jupiter square or opposite Ascendant, Jupiter Aquarius, Moon Jupiter, Venus Mars, Venus afflicted by Saturn, Uranus, Pluto, Mars or Neptune afflictions in Aquarius, Mars Jupiter, Sun or Moon in air; Pluto = Mars/Neptune; Saturn = Mars/Neptune, Sun + Venus – Mars = Ascendant

Blood donor: Moon MC

Blood fibrin: Mars, Jupiter, Pisces

Blood hemoglobin: Mars

Blood impurities: Mercury Jupiter, Mars Uranus, Mars Pluto, Jupiter Uranus

Blood loss: Mars Uranus

Blood plasma: Moon Neptune, Sun Jupiter

Blood poisoning: Mars Neptune in stress aspect, Mars Neptune Pluto, Aquarius emphasis, Pluto afflictions, Mars in Aquarius, Venus Pluto

Blood pressure, disorders: Moon Uranus, Sun Jupiter, Aries Libra

Blood pressure, high (hypertension): Moon Mars, Sun Mars, Moon Uranus, Jupiter afflictions

Blood pressure, low (hypotension): Aries Libra emphasis, Jupiter Saturn, Mars Saturn

Blood serum: Cancer

Blood sugar disorders: Venus afflicted, second house emphasis, Mars or Saturn in Virgo, fixed emphasis, Prominent Neptune, Venus Jupiter stress

11

Blood sugar balance: Libra
Blood sugar, high: Venus afflicted, Saturn in Virgo
Blood sugar, low: Venus Neptune, Venus Saturn
Blood transfusion: Sun Neptune Pluto
Blood transfusion, successful: Jupiter Pluto
Blood, venous: Venus
Bloody injury: Mars Uranus
Blows to body: Mars Saturn Pluto
Blushing: Moon Mars
Body: first house
Body abuse: Mars Neptune
Body acids: Mars
Body fluid: Moon, Cancer
Body containers: Cancer
Body heat: Sun
Body organs: Sun
Body outlets: Scorpio
Body, small: Sun Saturn
Body structure: Cancer Capricorn, Saturn
Body temperature: Mars, Sun
Body, weak: Sun Neptune
Boils: Mars in Taurus, Mars in Sagittarius, Mars in Capricorn, Mars Pluto
Bonding: Saturn
Bone disease: Saturn Neptune
Bone dislocation: Capricorn
Bone formation: Mars Saturn
Bone inflammation: Mars Saturn
Bone injury: Saturn Pluto
Bone malformation: Saturn Pluto
Bone marrow: Cancer

Bone marrow channels: Saturn Nodes

Bone meal tablets: Capricorn

Bones: Saturn, Capricorn

Bones, brittle: Saturn Ascendant

Bones, broken: Mars Saturn

Bones, disease of: Saturn affliction, Mars Saturn

Bones of face: Aries

Bone tissue: Sun Saturn

Bone weakness: Saturn

Bony system: Capricorn

Bowel cramps: Uranus

Bowel inflammation: Mars in Pisces, Mars in Virgo

Bowel irritation: Mercury Mars, Mars Uranus

Bowels: Scorpio

Bowels, septic: Saturn in Capricorn

Bowel trouble: Mercury or Virgo emphasis

Brain: Aries, Cancer, Libra, Taurus, Scorpio, first house

Brain, base: Taurus

Brain congestion: Aries

Brain damage: Aries

Brain disease: Aries, Mc = Sun/Neptune

Brain fever: Aries, Sun or Mars afflicted in Aries

Brain matter: Moon

Brain tumor: Saturn in first house, Saturn in Aries, Saturn MC, Saturn = Sun/MC, MC = Sun/Saturn. Sun = Saturn/MC

Breakage: Mars

Breast Bone: Cancer

Breast cancer: Cancer, Saturn in Cancer, fourth house emphasis, Jupiter in Cancer with Saturn, Saturn Cancer afflicted by Jupiter, Moon Pluto

Breasts: Cancer and Moon, fourth house, Venus

Breasts, cosmetically: Libra and Venus

Breasts, scanty milk production: Saturn in Cancer

Breath, bad: first house, Mercury Saturn, Taurus

Breathing: third house, Mercury, Gemini Sagittarius

Breathing, exhalation: Sagittarius

Breathing, inhalation: Gemini

Breathing, shallow: Saturn in Sagittarius

Bright's Disease: Saturn in Libra, Afflictions in Libra or Scorpio, Venus Mars stress

Brittleness: Saturn

Bronchials: Gemini

Bronchitis: Saturn in Gemini or Sagittarius, Venus Saturn affliction involving third house, prominent Taurus or Scorpio, Gemini emphasis or Mercury afflicted by Uranus, Neptune or Pluto

Brooding: Taurus

Bruises: Mars Saturn

Bulimia: Cancer, Saturn in fourth house

Bunions: Saturn in Pisces, twelfth house

Burial: fourth house

Burns: Sun Mars, Mars, Mars Jupiter, Mars Ascendant

Bursa: Cancer

Bursitis: Gemini

Buttocks: Libra, Mars in Libra

C

Cadaver: eighth house
Cadmium: Neptune
Caffeine: Neptune
Calf: Aquarius
Calcification: Saturn
Calcium deficiency: Saturn
Calculi: stones, Venus Saturn stress aspect
Cancer: weak Mars, lack of fire, Moon Saturn Jupiter and Neptune prominent, Saturn = Pluto/MC, Jupiter Saturn, Sun Saturn MC, Sun Saturn Pluto, Sun Saturn Neptune, Sun Neptune Pluto
Candida: Virgo, Venus Pluto
Capillaries: Gemini, Capricorn
Carbohydrate processes: Venus Jupiter
Carbohydrates: Venus
Carbon dioxide retention: Saturn in Aquarius
Carbuncles: Mars in Capricorn
Carcinoma: emphasized Moon or Cancer, Venus Saturn Jupiter afflictions, Sun Neptune, see also Cancer
Carcinoma, incurable: Pluto
Cardiac arrest: Sun Saturn, Mars Saturn
Cardiac arrhythmia: Uranus in Leo, Uranus prominent and afflicted, Aquarius emphasis

Cardiac embolism: Sun Uranus

Cardiac health: Sun

Cardiac hypertrophy: Sun Saturn

Cardiac insufficiency: Leo

Cardiac muscle: Mars Jupiter

Cardiac stress: Mars in Leo

Cardiomyopathy: Leo

Cardiovascular disorders: Sun Neptune or Sun Saturn stress, afflictions in Leo, Saturn in Leo, Malefics in fifth or eleventh house, Jupiter Saturn stress, Jupiter in Capricorn, Mars in Aquarius

Cardiovascular system: Sun Uranus, Leo Aquarius

Caries: Saturn Pluto

Carotid arteries: Taurus

Carpal Tunnel Syndrome: Mercury Saturn, Gemini

Cartilage: Capricorn, Saturn

Cartilage trouble: Capricorn

Cast: Cancer Capricorn

Castration: Scorpio

Catabolic processes: Mars Saturn

Catalepsy: Aries, Neptune in first house

Cataract: Neptune afflicting Mercury, Mars Jupiter in Virgo, Sun Moon in hard aspect, Saturn in Aquarius, Aries or Libra, Sun Saturn, Mercury Saturn

Catarrh: Cancer

Catarrh of bowel: Virgo

Catarrh of nasal passages: Scorpio

Catarrh of stomach: Cancer

Caustic: Mars

Cauterization: Mars

Cecum: Scorpio, Cancer

Celibacy: Saturn, Virgo

Cell division: Pluto

Cell division, abnormal: Uranus Pluto, Sun Pluto

Cell inflammation: Sun Mars

Cell nucleus: Sun

Cell nutrition: Jupiter

Cell regeneration: Jupiter, Sun Pluto

Cell replication: Pluto

Cell salts: Aries: Kali Phosphoricum; Taurus: Natrum Sulphuricum; Gemini: Kali Muriaticum; Cancer: Calcarea Flourica; Leo: Magnesia Phosphurica; Virgo: Kali Sulphuricum; Libra: Natrum Phosphori- cum; Scorpio: Calcarea Sulphurica; Sagittarius: Silicea; Capricorn: Calcarea Phosphorica; Aquarius: Natrum Muriaticum; Pisces: Ferrum Phosphoricum

Cellular exhaustion: Neptune

Cellulitis: Pluto

Cell walls: Capricorn

Cemeteries: Saturn, Capricorn, Pluto, Scorpio

Cemetery plot: fourth house, Moon

Centripetal: Sun Saturn

Cerebellum: Aries

Cerebral congestion: Aries

Cerebral embolism: Sun Uranus

Cerebral hemisphere of brain: Aries

Cerebral hemorrhage: Aries Libra axis, Uranus prominent and stress with Mars, planets in Aries

Cerebral meningitis: Aries, Neptune

Cerebral Palsy Mars Neptune, Mercury Uranus, Sun Saturn, Mercury Neptune, Aquarius

Cerebrum: Aries

Cesarean section: Pluto Ascendant, Mars Ascendant

Cesarean birth: Mars Ascendant, Mars Scorpio

Chastity: Virgo, Mars Neptune

Cheeks: Cancer

Chemical balance: Aries Libra

Chemical imbalance: Venus

Chemicals: Neptune

Chemical sensitivities: Neptune Pluto, Sun Neptune, Moon Neptune, Pisces emphasis

Chemotherapy: Neptune

Chest cavity: Cancer

Chest constriction: Saturn in Cancer

Chest disorders: Cancer

Chest pain: Jupiter Saturn, Jupiter Neptune, Gemini, Cancer

Chicken pox: Mars, Saturn, Pisces

Chilblains: Venus Saturn, Saturn in Gemini, Saturn in Pisces, Mars Saturn

Childbirth: Moon

Chills, colds: Saturn afflictions, Moon Saturn, Venus Saturn

Chin: Venus, Taurus

Chiropodist: Jupiter, Pisces

Chiropractor: Saturn, Capricorn

Chlorine: Mars

Chloroform: Neptune, Mercury Neptune

Chlorosis: Cancer, Mars in Cancer, Saturn in Cancer or Aries

Choking: Saturn in Taurus

Cholecystitis: Mercury Virgo, Jupiter Mars, Mars in Capricorn

Cholera: Mars in Virgo

Cholesterol: Sun Jupiter

Cholesterol deposit: Jupiter Saturn in hard aspect, Jupiter in Capricorn, Leo Aquarius or fifth and eleventh house emphasis

Choline: Jupiter

Chromium: Venus

18

Chronic: Saturn

Chronic disease: Saturn, fixed emphasis, Saturn Ascendant, Saturn Pluto, Jupiter Saturn

Chronic Fatigue Syndrome: Sun Saturn, Sun Neptune, Mars Neptune, angular and afflicted, Moon Neptune, weak fire, Mars afflicted, twelfth house emphasis

Chronic health problems: twelfth house

Chyle: Moon, Virgo

Chylification: Virgo

Chymification: Cancer

Circulation: Venus Jupiter, Aquarius, Leo, Sun, fifth and eleventh houses

Circulation, poor: Venus Aquarius afflicted, Jupiter afflicted, Saturn in Aquarius, Saturn = Sun/Neptune

Circulation, stoppage: Saturn, Venus Saturn

Circulatory disorders: afflictions to Sun, Leo Aquarius, fifth and eleventh house emphasis, Saturn in Aquarius, Venus Uranus, Saturn Uranus, Mars Uranus, Uranus afflicted, fixed emphasis, Saturn Uranus

Circulatory system: Leo Aquarius, fifth and eleventh houses and their rulers

Cirrhoses: Jupiter Saturn

Cirrhoses of the liver: Jupiter conjunct Saturn, Mercury Saturn, Sagittarius

Claudication: Mars in Aquarius, Saturn in Sagittarius

Claustrophobia: Saturn Neptune

Clavicles: Gemini

Cleft palate: Aries

Clitoris: Scorpio

Club foot: Saturn in Aquarius, Pluto

Coagulate: Venus Saturn, Jupiter Saturn, Mars Saturn

Cobalamin: Mars

Cobalt: Mars

Coccyx: Scorpio

Cochlear: Taurus

Cognition: Moon Pluto, Mercury

Cold: Saturn

Colds: Mercury Saturn, Sun Moon

Cold sweat: Aries, Libra, Scorpio combined with Moon, Saturn, Venus, Mars, and Neptune

Colic: Jupiter Uranus, Virgo

Colisepsis: Mars Neptune, Taurus Scorpio

Colitis: eighth house emphasis, Pluto angular, Uranus in Cancer, Virgo or Mercury emphasis, Mercury Saturn, Saturn in Virgo, afflictions in Scorpio, especially Mars, Mars in Scorpio, Mars or Pluto in stress aspect to Sun, Moon, or Ascendant, Mars or Saturn in Scorpio, Neptune = Mercury/Mars

Collagen: Gemini, Saturn in Gemini

Collarbone: Gemini

Colon: Scorpio

Colon, aid: Mars in Scorpio

Colon disorders: Scorpio emphasis, eighth house emphasis, Mercury Mars stress, Mars Pluto stress, Mars Uranus stress, fixed emphasis, Mars or Saturn in Scorpio

Colonic: Scorpio, Virgo

Colon stasis: Saturn in Taurus or Scorpio

Color blindness: Prominent Moon Neptune

Colostomy: Mars Pluto

Coma: Neptune afflicted, Uranus square or opposite Neptune, Neptune in eighth house, afflictions in Aries or Libra, Jupiter afflicted in Libra

Comatose: Neptune

Complexes: Moon Saturn

Complexion: Venus Ascendant

Compulsive eating: Jupiter Pluto

Compulsiveness: Taurus, excess earth

Conceit: Jupiter

Conception: Venus Uranus, Moon Venus, Scorpio, fourth house, Moon

Concussion: Aries

Condensation: Saturn

Confidence: Leo

Confinement: Neptune, twelfth house

Confusion: Saturn Neptune

Congenital disorder: Nodes

Congenital heart disease: Saturn Venus afflictions, fixed emphasis, see also Heart

Congestion: Moon Saturn, Saturn, Sun Neptune

Conjunctiva: Cancer

Conjunctivitis: Mars in Cancer, Moon Pluto

Connective tissue: Gemini, Nodes, Saturn

Connectivity: Gemini, Nodes

Consciousness: cadent houses, Aries

Consciousness, loss of: Moon Neptune, Mercury Neptune, Saturn MC

Consciousness, disturbance of: Moon Neptune

Constipation: Saturn in Virgo or Scorpio, Mercury Saturn, Capricorn, Mars Saturn, Saturn in Taurus or Scorpio, Mars in Scorpio

Constitution: Sun

Consumptive: Saturn in Gemini, Saturn Neptune

Contagious infection: Neptune Nodes

Containingness: Cancer

Contamination: Mars Neptune

Continence: Saturn in Virgo, Moon Saturn

Contortion: Uranus
Contraction: Saturn, Saturn Uranus
Contrariness: Uranus
Contraception pill: Pluto
Contractions: Moon Uranus
Contracting: Saturn
Contrariness: Uranus
Convalescence: Pluto Ascendant
Convulsions: Uranus, Prominent Mercury Mars, Moon Mars
  Uranus
Coordination: Mercury
Copper: Venus, Mars
Cornea: Cancer
Corns: Pisces
Coronary arteries: Leo
Coronary thrombosis: Saturn, Mars or Saturn in Scorpio, Sun
  Moon afflictions with Uranus and sign Taurus or Scorpio,
  Leo afflictions, Venus Jupiter afflictions
Corpulent: Jupiter
Corpuscles, red: Mars
Corpuscles, white: Neptune
Cosmetic surgery: Venus Libra or Scorpio, Mars Scorpio, Ar-
  ies, eighth house, Pluto
Cough: Taurus Scorpio afflictions, Mars in Gemini
Coverings: Cancer
Cramps: Jupiter Uranus, Uranus Ascendant, Mercury Mars,
  Aquarius
Cranium: Aries, Saturn
Cravings: Neptune Ascendant
Crepitation: Saturn in Taurus
Crippling: Uranus
Crib death: Saturn Mercury and involvement of third house

Cripple: Sun Mars, Mars Saturn, Moon Mars, Mars Ascendant

Crohn's Disease: eighth house emphasis, Mars Uranus, Scorpio emphasis, prominent Pluto, Neptune in Scorpio, Mars Pluto

Croup: Saturn in Taurus

Cruelty: Mars Saturn, Mars Uranus, Gemini, prominent Mars

Cryogenics: Saturn, Capricorn

Crystallization: Saturn

CT scan: Uranus, Aries

Cure: Jupiter Ascendant

Cushing's Syndrome: Mars in Aries, Saturn in Aries

Cutaneous eruptions: Mars

Cutaneous eruptions on the face: Aries

Cuticles: Capricorn

Cutting: Mars

Cuts: Mars Aries

Cuts of arms, hands and collarbone: Mars Gemini

Cyrogenics: Saturn, Capricorn

Cyst: Jupiter afflictions in water, Pisces, Taurus

Cystitis: Mars in Scorpio, Libra

D

Daily rhythms: Moon

Deafness: Moon Saturn affliction, Saturn prominent and afflicted and debilitated Moon, Saturn Aries, Mercury Saturn, Capricorn, see also Hearing

Death: eighth house, Saturn, Pluto, Scorpio

Debility: Saturn, Neptune = Sun/Mars

Decomposition: Saturn Neptune, Pluto, Mars Pluto

Defense system: Mars

Defensiveness: Saturn

Deformity: Saturn,

Degenerative disease: Saturn Pluto, Saturn Neptune

Degeneration: Saturn Uranus Neptune, Pluto MC

Dehydration: Mars in Aries, Leo, excess fire, low water

Dejection: Saturn

Delirium: Mercury Neptune, Mars Neptune

Delirium Tremens: Mercury Uranus Neptune combination

Delusion: Mercury Neptune, Neptune

Dementia: Moon Mercury afflicted

Demulcent: Venus Jupiter

Dengue Fever: Mars, Venus Mars afflictions, Mars Saturn

Dental problems: Saturn Ascendant

Dentists: sixth house, Mars

Dentures: Mars Pluto, Neptune

Depression: Saturn or Capricorn emphasis, Saturn in first, third or sixth house afflicted, Saturn afflicted in Virgo, Mercury afflicted in Aries, Moon Neptune, Mercury Saturn, Venus Saturn, Moon Saturn, Saturn MC, Mercury Pluto, Saturn Neptune, Saturn = Sun/MC, Saturn signs, Pluto = Moon/Saturn, Moon = Saturn/MC, Mars = Saturn/Neptune, Moon = Saturn/Neptune

Depressive psychosis: Neptune MC, Mercury = Neptune/MC

Derma: Saturn

Dermatitis: Libra, Venus

Desire body: Mars

Despondency: Capricorn

Destroy: Pluto

Detoxification: Pluto, Jupiter, Sun Neptune

Dexterity: Mercury Mars, Good aspects to Mercury or Gemini

Diabetes: Venus, Sun Uranus afflictions, Jupiter Uranus afflictions, Venus Saturn Neptune combination, Mercury Mars stress aspect, second house emphasis, Venus in Cancer or Taurus afflicted, fixed emphasis, stress aspects from Mars or Pluto, Saturn in Virgo, Venus Jupiter aspect, Saturn Neptune afflicting Jupiter; Jupiter = Mars/Pluto

Diagnosis, correct: Jupiter Ascendant

Diagnosis, positive: Mercury Jupiter

Diagnosis, technical equipment: Jupiter Uranus

Diaphragm: Cancer

Diarrhea: Virgo

Diet: Cancer, sixth house

Dietary habits: sixth house

Dietician: sixth house, Mercury

Diffusion: Neptune

Digestion: Fire, Moon, Virgo Pisces, fourth house

Digestive disturbances: Moon Venus, Moon Mars, afflictions in Cancer, Mars or Saturn in Cancer in hard aspect to Sun,

Moon or Ascendant

Digestive juices: Cancer

Digestive juices, release of: Virgo

Dimples: Venus

Diphtheria: Taurus Scorpio, twelfth house, Moon Saturn

Dipsomania: Moon Cancer

Discharges: Moon

Disabilities, body: Saturn

Disabilities, mental: Mercury

Discontent: Saturn afflicting Moon or Venus and involvement of third house, Venus afflicted by Mars, Venus square Saturn

Discipline: Capricorn

Discontent: Moon Saturn Venus combination, Venus square Saturn

Discrimination: Virgo Pisces

Disease, acute: Mars

Disease, bites or stings: Neptune

Disease caused by excess: Jupiter

Disease caused by wrong diet: Saturn in Cancer

Disease commencement: Pluto Ascendant

Disease, lingering: Neptune Pluto, Saturn, Saturn = Sun/Neptune

Disease, rare: Uranus

Disease, sexually transmitted: eighth house

Disease, short: Sun Jupiter

Disease, violent: Mars in Aries

Disease, wasting: Neptune

Disfigurement: Saturn

Disintegration: Pluto

Dislocation: Capricorn

Dismembering: Mars

Disorientation: Sun Neptune, Jupiter Neptune

Dispersal: Gemini

Dissemination: Neptune

Dissipation: Neptune, Pluto

Dissolve: Neptune

Distention: Mars Jupiter

Distillation: Libra, Venus

Distributive function: Gemini Sagittarius

Diuretic: Moon

Diverticulitis: Scorpio, eighth house emphasis, Mars Pluto

Dizziness: Mercury Jupiter, Mars Neptune, Aries

DNA: Pluto

Doctor: Scorpio

Dorsal vertebrae: Leo

Down's Syndrome: Sun Saturn, Mercury Mars in twelfth, Mercury R, Mars in Mercury sign or Mercury in Mars sign, Mercury Mars, Mercury/Mars = twelfth house ruler

Dreaming: Mercury Neptune

Dropsy: Saturn in Libra, Moon Venus, Sun Neptune, Moon prominent and afflicted

Drowning: Moon, Neptune

Drug addiction: Moon Neptune, Sun Neptune, Pluto angular, Sun = Neptune/Pluto

Drugs: Neptune

Drug reaction: Uranus Neptune, Neptune Pluto

Drug sensitivity: Neptune, Sun Neptune, Moon Neptune, Venus Neptune, Mars Neptune

Dry cough: Mercury

Dryness: Aries, Saturn, Capricorn

Ductless glands: Neptune

Duodenal ulcer: Mars in Virgo or Pisces in stress aspect to Sun, Moon, Saturn, Uranus or Neptune

Duodenitis: Virgo

Duodenum: Virgo Pisces
Duodenum trouble: afflictions involving Mercury or Virgo
Ducts: Gemini
Dwarfism: Sun Saturn
Dysentery: Mars in Virgo
Dysfunction: Pluto
Dyslexia: Mercury Saturn
Dysmenorrhoea: Saturn in Scorpio, Mars in Scorpio
Dyspareunia: Mars in eighth, Saturn in Scorpio, Mars Pluto
Dyspepsia: Mars in Pisces, Cancer
Dysphasia: Saturn in Gemini, Mercury Saturn, Saturn in Aries
Dysplasia: Pluto
Dystrophy: Pluto, Saturn in Cancer

E

Ear abscesses: Mars in Taurus

Earaches: Saturn Aries, Taurus

Ear discharge: Mars in Libra

Ear, middle: Taurus

Ear, middle inflammation: Saturn Ascendant

Ear, nose, throat doctor: Taurus

Ears: Taurus, Mercury

Ears, outer: Aries

Ear trouble: Saturn stress aspect to planet or angle, Mercury Uranus, Saturn Ascendant, Moon Saturn

Eating disorders: Taurus, Cancer, fourth and tenth houses

Eating habits: Mercury

Eccentricity: Uranus

Eclampsia: Pluto Nodes

Eczema: Capricorn emphasis, afflictions in Libra or Capricorn, Venus Aries afflicted, Mars Neptune afflictions, Venus and/ or Libra in poor cosmic state, Saturn afflicting Ascendant, Venus Saturn stress aspect, prominent and afflicted Venus, 15o Libra.

Edema: Sun Neptune, Moon

Ego: Sun, MC

Ego, weak: Sun poorly placed, Mars Neptune, Mars in twelfth house, Neptune in first house

Ejaculation: Mars
Ejection: Scorpio
Elbows: Cancer Capricorn
Electrical accidents: Mars Uranus
Electrical procedures: Uranus
Electrical therapies: Saturn Uranus, Uranus Neptune
Electricity: Uranus
Electrolytes: Uranus, Neptune
Electromagnetism: Uranus
Elimination: Taurus Scorpio, Libra
Eliminative function: Taurus Scorpio
Elusive: Neptune
Emaciation: Saturn
Embolism: Jupiter Saturn
Embolus: Saturn
Embryo: Moon
Embryonic growth: Pluto Nodes
Emetic: Moon, Venus
Emollient: Jupiter
Emotional confusion: Venus Neptune
Emotional disorders: Moon
Emotional illness: Moon Saturn, Moon Uranus, Saturn = Pluto/Ascendant
Emotionalism: Fire and Water, Moon Uranus
Emotionally caused disease: Moon = Sun/Saturn
Emotionally cold: Saturn
Emotional shock: Uranus = Saturn/MC, Moon Uranus
Emotional stress: Mars Ascendant, Moon Mars
Emotional suffering: Saturn = Neptune/Pluto
Emotional vitality: Sun Moon
Emotions: Moon

Emotions affect health: Moon = Sun/Saturn

Emphysema: Uranus, Saturn in Gemini, Mercury Saturn Jupiter

Enema: Scorpio

Encephalitis: Aries, Mars in Aries afflicted, Mercury afflicted, Venus afflicted in Aries

Endocardium: Cancer

Endocartitis: Mars in Leo, Cancer

Endocrine disorders: Uranus Pluto, Mercury Pluto, Neptune Pluto, Pluto = Moon/Mars

Endocrine dysfunction: Sun Pluto, Sun Saturn

Endocrine system: Pluto

End of life: fourth house

Endurance: Taurus, fixed signs, Saturn

Energy: Leo, Sun, Mars

Energy blockage: Saturn = Mars/Uranus

Energy depletion: Neptune, Sun Saturn

Energy problems: Sun stress aspect, Mars Saturn, Mars Neptune

Engorgement: Mars Jupiter, Jupiter

Engorgement and venous stasis: Venus Jupiter afflictions

Enlargement: Jupiter

Enteric fever: Mars Saturn, Virgo, Mutability

Enteritis: Virgo, Mars in Virgo

Environmental stress: Mars Ascendant

Environmental toxins/allergies: Saturn/Neptune = Ascendant or MC

Enzyme action: Virgo, Jupiter, Pluto

Enzymes: Pluto

Epidemic: Jupiter Saturn, Saturn Neptune, Mars Neptune

Epidermis: Capricorn

Epigastria: Cancer

Epilepsy: Uranus prominent, Mercury cadent and afflicted by Mars, Saturn or Uranus, Mercury stress Uranus, Uranus in third house; Sun = Uranus/Neptune, Uranus = Moon/Venus, Uranus = Sun/Neptune

Episiotomy: Mars Ascendant, Mars in Scorpio

Epstein-Barr virus syndrome: Pluto, Neptune = Sun/Moon, twelfth house emphasis, Mars Neptune, Mars Pluto

Erotic desires: Mars = Venus/Neptune

Eruption: Pluto, Mars

Erysipelas: Mars, Venus Mars Jupiter

Escapism: Pisces, Neptune

Esophagus: Taurus Cancer

Esophagus, lower: Cancer

Esophagus, upper: Taurus

Estrogen: Venus Mars

Ether: Neptune, Aquarius

Eustachian tube: Gemini, Taurus, Venus

Excesses: Venus Jupiter, Mars Jupiter

Excretory organs: Scorpio

Exercise: Mars

Exhaustion: Mars Ascendant

Exophthalmia goiter: Sun Uranus, Venus afflictions

Exoscosis: Capricorn

Explosive: Uranus

Extroversion: upper hemisphere, positive signs

Eyeballs: Aries

Eyebrows: Aries

Eye disease: Sun Neptune, Sun Moon, Moon Neptune

Eye disorders: Sun Moon, Aries Libra, Neptune in aspect to Sun or Moon, afflictions in center of mutable signs, Moon Mars, 29° Taurus, 9° Sagittarius, 29° Sagittarius

Eye glasses: Moon Mercury Neptune

Eye-hand coordination: Mercury
Eye problems: Sun
Eyes: Sun Moon, Aries, Uranus, Aquarius, see also Sight
Eyes, left eye of female: Sun
Eyes, left eye of male: Moon
Eyes, right eye of female: Moon
Eyes, right eye of male: Sun
Eye strain: Jupiter Neptune
Eye sockets: Cancer

F

Face: first house, Aries, Mars

Face, diseases of: first house, Aries, Mars

Face flushes: Aries

Face injuries: Mars

Facial neuralgia: Aries, Mercury in Aries

Facial pain: Mercury Uranus, Mercury in Aries, Mercury Mars

Facial swelling: Venus in Aries

Facial surgery: Aries

Failure: Saturn

Fainting: Sun or Leo planets afflicted, Neptune or Pluto afflicted

Fallopian tube: Gemini, Scorpio

Falls: Mars Saturn, Capricorn

Fanatical: Moon Pluto

Fantasy: Neptune

Fasting: Saturn, Saturn = Sun./Pluto

Fat: Jupiter

Fat assimilation: Jupiter

Fat disposition: Jupiter

Father complex: Saturn Retrograde, Sun Saturn

Fatigue: Mars Neptune, Sun Neptune

Fatty acids: Mars Jupiter

Fatty degeneration: Jupiter

Fear: Moon Neptune, Mercury Saturn, Mercury Neptune

Feces: Saturn, Pluto, Scorpio

Feeble: Sun Saturn

Feet: Pisces

Feet, cold: Saturn in Pisces

Feet, deformed: twelfth house, Jupiter, Neptune, Pisces

Feet, flat: Pisces

Feet, sweating: Mars in Pisces

Female diseases: Moon and Venus afflictions

Female glands: Moon Venus

Female organ dysfunction: Venus Neptune

Female reproductive glands: Venus Pluto

Female trouble: Venus afflicted, afflictions in Libra or Scorpio, Venus Neptune

Femoral artery: Sagittarius

Femur: Sagittarius

Fertility: Cancer, Scorpio, Pisces, water emphasis, Moon, fifth and eleventh houses

Fertility, low: Venus = Mars/Neptune

Festering disease: Saturn, See also Disease

Fetus: Cancer

Fever: Mars, Sun Mars, Sun Moon, Aries, Leo, Sagittarius

Fever, massive: Mars Pluto

Fibrillation: Uranus prominent and afflicted, Aquarius emphasis

Fibrin: Mars, Jupiter, Pisces

Fibroid tumor: Moon Pluto, Saturn in Cancer, Saturn afflicted in Scorpio, Saturn conjunct Moon in Scorpio, Mars conjunct Venus, malefics in Taurus or Scorpio

Fibula: Aquarius

Fingers: Gemini, third house

Filtration: Libra, Venus

Fingernails: Saturn

Fingers: Gemini, third house

Firearms: Mars

Fistulas: Taurus Scorpio

Fits: Uranus, Jupiter Uranus, Moon Mars Uranus

Flabbiness: Moon Jupiter

Flaccidity: Pisces

Flanks: Sagittarius

Flare-ups: Mars

Flatulency: Cancer

Flesh: Venus

Flexibility: Gemini

Fluid Balance: Moon

Fluorine: Saturn

Folic Acid: Mars

Food consumption: Taurus Scorpio

Food sensitivities: Mercury Uranus, Moon, Cancer, Moon
Neptune

Foot injury: Mars in Pisces

Foot trouble: afflicted planets in Pisces or prominent and afflicted Neptune

Forceps at birth: Mars Ascendant

Forehead: Aries

Fractures: Mars in Sagittarius, Mars Saturn

Fractures of arms, hands or collarbone: Mars in Gemini

Frames: Saturn

Frenzy: Aries, Mars

Frigidity: Saturn

Fructose: Venus

Functional disorders: Moon, sixth house

Fungus growth: prominent and afflicted Neptune, Saturn
Neptune, Sun Neptune, Neptune Ascendant, Neptune
Nodes

G

Gallbladder: Cancer, Saturn, Jupiter Saturn, Planets in Capricorn, Capricorn on sixth house cusp

Gallbladder inflammation: Mars in Capricorn

Gallbladder, sluggish: Saturn in Capricorn, Jupiter stress Saturn

Gallstones: Mars and Saturn prominent and afflicted, Mars or Saturn in Cancer or Capricorn, Saturn = Moon/Jupiter

Ganglion (nerves): Mercury

Ganglion (cyst): Mercury, Taurus

Gangrene: Mars Pluto afflictions, Venus Mars afflictions, afflictions involving Saturn, Neptune or Pluto

Gas: air, Aquarius, Neptune

Gas in stomach: Cancer

Gastric ailments: Cancer

Gastric mucous: Cancer

Gastric ulcer: Mars or Saturn in Cancer, Moon Mars, Mars in Libra or Aries

Gastritis: Sun in Virgo, Moon afflicted and involvement of Mars and planets in Cancer

Gastroenteritis: Mars in Virgo, Mars in Cancer, Mercury Mars

Gel: Saturn, Moon

Genetic disorders: Pluto Ascendant

Genital disorders: Pluto

Genitals: Pluto, Scorpio, Mars, eighth house

Genius: Uranus

Germs: Pluto

Gestation: Moon

Giant: Pluto

Giddiness: Aries

Gingivitis: Taurus

Glandular atrophy: Venus Saturn

Glandular malfunction: Moon Saturn, Mars Pluto, Neptune Pluto, Venus Neptune, Venus = Saturn/Neptune, Venus = Mars/Uranus, Saturn = Moon/Venus, Neptune = Moon/Venus, Uranus = Moon/Venus, Sun = Venus/Saturn

Glandular secretions: Mercury Venus, Venus Jupiter

Glandular swellings: Pisces, Neptune

Glandular swellings in neck: Taurus, Venus

Glandular system: Mercury Pluto

Glaucoma: Aries Aquarius, Sun afflicted, Cancer

Gloom: Saturn

Glucose: Venus

Glucose metabolism: Venus Jupiter

Glucose, overproduction: Venus Neptune, Jupiter Neptune

Gluten allergy: Virgo

Gluteus muscles: Sagittarius

Gluttony: Jupiter Ascendant, Moon Taurus, Venus in Taurus or Cancer aspecting Mars

Glycogen: Venus, Libra, Jupiter

Glycogen balance: Venus Jupiter

Glycosuria: Venus in Scorpio

Goiter: Taurus and Leo afflictions, Jupiter Neptune, Venus Saturn

Gold: Sun

Gonads: Scorpio

Gonorrhea: Mars Leo in eighth house square Moon, Venus Mars afflicted, water emphasis, Scorpio emphasis, Venus = Mars/Neptune, Saturn = Sun Venus, Neptune = Venus/Mars

Gourmandizing: Jupiter

Gout: prominent Jupiter, Venus Sagittarius, Venus and fifth house connection, Sun Jupiter, Mercury Mars, Saturn in Sagittarius, Sagittarius or Pisces emphasis

Graphite: Saturn

Gravel: Scorpio, Saturn

Graves Disease: Sun Uranus, Venus afflicted

Groin: Scorpio, Pluto

Growths: Jupiter

Guilt: Saturn, Saturn Moon

Gum boils: Aries

Gum disease: Saturn in Taurus

Gums: Taurus

Gums, lower: Taurus

Gums, upper: Aries

Gunshot: Sun Mars affliction

Gynecological disorders: Venus Mars stress, Venus or Mars in Scorpio, Moon Mars, Moon Venus, afflictions in Cancer or Scorpio, Moon afflicted, Venus Saturn stress, Venus Neptune stress, Venus = Mars/Pluto, Neptune = Moon/Mars. Saturn = Moon/Venus, Pluto = Moon/Venus

H

Habits: Moon

Hair: Capricorn

Hair loss: Saturn

Halitosis: Taurus, Mercury Saturn, first house

Hallucination: Pisces, Neptune, Moon Neptune, Mercury Neptune, Jupiter Neptune

Hamstrings: Mars Jupiter, Sagittarius

Handicap: Sun Saturn

Hands: Gemini, Mercury

Hands, swollen: Moon in Gemini

Hardening: Saturn

Harelip: Aries

Hay fever: predominance of mutability, prominent and afflicted Mercury, Gemini or Sagittarius emphasis, Mercury Saturn aspect, prominent Neptune, Sun Gemini, Moon afflicted in Taurus or Scorpio

Head: Aries

Headache: Mars in Aries or Libra, Saturn in Aries or Libra, afflictions involving Aries, Ascendant, Moon and Mars, hard aspect from Mars and planets in Aries involved, Mercury Jupiter, Mercury Uranus, Uranus Ascendant

Head injuries: Mars in first house, Aries emphasis, Moon in Aries

Healer: Pisces

Healer, faith: angular Uranus or Neptune

Healer, magnetic: fixed and earth emphasis, Mercury Uranus, Mercury Neptune

Healing crises: eighth house

Healing hands: Gemini, Uranus in eighth house

Healing powers: Scorpio, Angular Chiron, Mercury Uranus, Mercury Neptune

Health: first house, Sun, sixth house

Health foods: sixth house, Mercury

Health, good: Sun Jupiter, Jupiter MC, Mars = Sun/Jupiter

Health matters: sixth

Health of men: Sun

Health of women: Moon

Health, poor: Sun Saturn, Sun Neptune, Saturn MC

Hearing: third house, Aries, Mercury, Gemini, see also Ears

Hearing aid: Uranus, sixth house, Neptune

Hearing, deficiency: twelfth house afflictions, Saturn in Gemini, Saturn in twelfth house, Saturn in Mercury house, Saturn in sixth or eighth house, Mercury stress aspect to Uranus, Moon in hard aspect to Mercury in twelfth, Virgo emphasis, Mercury in Capricorn afflicted

Hearing, loss of: Mars and Saturn afflicting Mercury and in-volvement of Gemini, Sagittarius or Pisces, Mars or Saturn in twelfth house

Hearing organs: Mercury Saturn

Heart attack: Mars in Leo, Sun Mars Uranus, Mars Saturn Uranus

Heart block: Mars Saturn, Saturn Uranus

Heartburn: Mars in Cancer or Capricorn, Moon in Leo

Heart condition: Sun Jupiter, Sun Neptune

Heart disease: Leo Aquarius, Sun afflicted, Sun Mars Uranus in affliction to Sun or Moon, afflictions to fifth house, malefics in or ruling fifth or eleventh, fixed emphasis, Saturn in Leo

Heart failure: Mars in Aquarius, Uranus Neptune

Heart membrane: Cancer

Heart murmur: Venus Uranus

Heart muscle: Leo, Mars Jupiter

Heart palpitations: Aquarius, Taurus or Scorpio emphasis, Sun Uranus, Mars in Leo. Uranus in Leo, Aquarius, Taurus or Scorpio, Sun Jupiter, Sun Mars

Heart, pumping action of: Leo

Heart valves: Aquarius, Uranus, Cancer

Heat: Mars

Helplessness: Moon Venus Neptune combination, Saturn in twelfth house, Saturn afflictions, lack of cardinality

Hematuria: Mars in Scorpio

Hemoglobin: Mars

Hemolysis: Jupiter Neptune, Mars Saturn

Hemophilia: malefics in second-eighth axis, Mars Saturn stress aspect, Jupiter afflictions, afflictions to Sun, Moon or Ascendant

Hemorrhaging: Moon Mars

Hemorrhoids: Mars or Saturn in Scorpio, Uranus Scorpio stress to Sun or Moon, Jupiter Scorpio or Jupiter stress to planets in Scorpio, eighth house emphasis, Venus = Mars/ Pluto

Hepatic system: Jupiter, Sagittarius, ninth house

Hepatitis: Saturn in Sagittarius, Mars in Sagittarius, Jupiter Saturn (see also Immune Deficient for more information)

Herbal treatment: Neptune, Venus

Heredity: Sun and Moon, fourth and tenth houses, Moon Saturn, Saturn Ascendant

Hereditary disease: Pluto, Moon Saturn, Pluto = Moon/Saturn

Hereditary weakness: Saturn Neptune, Uranus Neptune

Hernia: Mars Saturn Virgo Scorpio combination

Hernia, inguinal and scrotal: Mars in Scorpio, Mars Saturn, Venus Mars

Herpes: Mars, Venus Pluto, Uranus, Neptune or Pluto prominent and afflicted, Venus and Mercury afflicted

Hiatus hernia: Saturn in Leo, Moon Uranus, Moon Mars

Hiccoughs: Aquarius, Cancer

Hidden illness: Neptune,

High blood pressure: Moon Mars, Jupiter, Mars Jupiter in stress aspect, Saturn in Leo conjunct Jupiter, Saturn conjunct Jupiter or Venus, Uranus Ascendant, Mars in Leo

High strung: Mercury Mars, Mercury Uranus

Hindrance: Saturn

Hip disease: Sagittarius

Hip dislocation: Saturn in Sagittarius

Hip inflammation: Mars in Sagittarius

Hip injury: Mars in Sagittarius

Hip joint disease: Saturn in Sagittarius

Hips: Sagittarius

Hip surgery: Mars Jupiter

Histamine: Neptune

H.I.V.: Mars Neptune, Neptune Pluto, Pisces, twelfth house

Hives: Mars, Sun Mars, Venus afflicted, prominent and afflicted Moon, Moon Mars, Capricorn

Hoarseness: Taurus, Venus Saturn

Hodgkin's Disease: Jupiter in Pisces, Saturn Neptune

Homeostasis: Venus, Libra

Homicidal tendency: afflictions to Sun, Leo, and Aries, Sun, Moon or malefics afflicting Ascendant, Venus Uranus, Taurus

Hopelessness: Moon Saturn Neptune

Hormonal imbalance: Mercury,

Hormonal imbalance, female: Neptune = Moon/Venus, Saturn = Moon/Venus

Hormone metabolism: Venus Jupiter

Hormones: Mercury

Homosexuality: Uranus

Hospitalization: Nodes, twelfth house, Node or Ascendant = Sun/Neptune, Nodes = Mars/Neptune

Hospitals: twelfth house, Neptune, Pisces

Humerus: Gemini

Hydrochloric acid: Mars

Hydrochloric, acid: excess: Mars in Cancer

Hydrochloric acid, lack: Saturn in Cancer

Hygiene: sixth house, Virgo

Hyperactivity: Mars

Hyperemia: Jupiter, Mars Jupiter

Hyperglycemia: Venus Jupiter, Neptune prominent, Virgo emphasis, fixed emphasis

Hyperinsulinism: Mars in Virgo, Mars in Pisces

Hyperopia: Sun Moon

Hypersensitivity: Mercury Neptune

Hypertension: Mars afflicted in cardinal sign, Sun Uranus

Hyperthyroidism: Mars in Taurus

Hypertonic: Mars

Hypertrophy: Saturn

Hypnotists: twelfth House, Neptune

Hypnotherapist: Angular Uranus or Neptune

Hypoactivity: Saturn

Hypochondria: Saturn, Jupiter Neptune, Virgo

Hypodermic needle: Mars

Hypoglycemia: Afflictions to Mars, Venus afflicted, Venus Jupiter stress, Mars in Virgo, Mars Jupiter Neptune, Jupiter

= Mars/Neptune, Moon = Jupiter/Neptune
Hysterectomy: Pluto in eighth square fifth house cusp
Hysteria: Sun Uranus, Gemini

I

Ileitis: Virgo, Scorpio

Iliac: Sagittarius

Ileum: Sagittarius, Virgo

Illness, chronic: Saturn

Illness, lingering: Saturn Neptune,

Illusionary: Neptune

Imbalance: Sun Moon or Venus with Uranus

Immobility: Saturn

Immune deficient: Saturn in Pisces, Mars Neptune, Mars Saturn, Sun Neptune, Jupiter Neptune, twelfth house emphasis, Mars in Pisces, weak Mars, Sun or Moon afflicted by Saturn or Neptune, mutable emphasis, Sun = Mars/Saturn, Neptune = Sun/Mars, Neptune = Sun/Moon, MC = Mars/ Neptune

Immune system: Neptune

Immunity: Sun in Aries or Leo well-aspected, Angular Mars or Jupiter

Immunoglobulins: Neptune, Pluto

Immunosuppression: Saturn Neptune

Impatience: Mars, Moon Aries, Sun Mars, Moon Mars

Impediment: Saturn

Impetigo: Capricorn, Venus Mars afflicted

Impetuous: Mars

Impotence: Mars Saturn, Venus in Pisces, Venus Neptune, Mars = Sun/Neptune

Impregnation: Moon

Impulsive: Mars

Inconstancy: Moon

Incontinence: Scorpio

Incoordination: Uranus, Mercury Uranus

Incubation: Neptune Ascendant

Incurable disease: Uranus, Pisces

Indecision: Mars Saturn

Indigestion: Mars, Saturn, Uranus or Neptune in Cancer, Mars in Pisces, afflicted Moon, Mercury in Virgo, Moon or Mercury in Cancer or Virgo in stress aspect, afflictions in Virgo especially if Mercury involved, 2-5o Virgo-Pisces, excess air

Indulgence: Venus

Inertia: Saturn

Infantile paralysis: See Poliomyelitis, Sun, Mars, Uranus, Saturn prominent

Infant mortality: Mutable afflictions, Negative signs, afflictions involving Cancer or Leo, Moon in stress aspect, Sun, Moon, Ascendant combination in stress aspect

Infection: Mars, Mars + Neptune, Mars in Pisces, Sun Neptune, Mars Neptune, Jupiter Neptune, Neptune = Jupiter/Pluto

Infection, massive: Mars Pluto

Infectious disease: Mars Neptune, Neptune with Mars Pluto

Inferiority complex: Saturn afflicted with third house, Virgo or Neptune emphasis, Sun Saturn, Saturn Neptune

Infirmary: twelfth house, Neptune

Infirmity: Sun Neptune

Infertility: Weak Saturn, Libra and Pisces, Mars Saturn

Inflammation: Sun, Mars, Mercury Mars, Sun Mars, Mars Pluto

Influenza: Jupiter Saturn, Mercury Mars Neptune prominent, Taurus Scorpio

Ingestion: Taurus Cancer

Inherited conditions: Nodes (see also Heredity)

Inhibition: Capricorn, Saturn

Injury: Mars Uranus, Mars Pluto, Mars Saturn, eighth house

Injury, self inflicted: Pisces

Injury through animals: sixth house

Inositol: Jupiter

Insanity: twelfth house afflictions, Mars in third house in water sign, Moon and Mercury stress aspect to Mars or Uranus, Mars afflicting ruler of third house

Insect bites: Mars Pluto, Uranus Neptune

Insect poisoning: Pluto

Insect stings: Mars

Insidious: Neptune

Insomnia: Aries, afflictions from Sun, Mars, Uranus, afflictions to twelfth house from planet in a cadent house, Moon Mercury stress and involvement of cadent houses, Mars or Uranus rising and afflicting the Ascendant, Neptune Nodes, Mercury Mars:

Instincts: Moon

Insulin secretion: Venus

Intelligence: Mercury, Gemini Virgo, Moon Mercury, Ascendant well-aspected

Intercostal pain: Gemini, Mars Cancer

Intestinal cramps: Virgo, Uranus

Intestinal disorders: Mars or Saturn in Virgo or Pisces, mutability, Virgo rising or on cusp of sixth house, afflictions to Sun or Moon in Virgo or Pisces, Mercury Venus, Mercury Mars, Mercury Jupiter, Jupiter Uranus

Intestinal stasis: Saturn in Virgo

Intestines, large: Scorpio

Intestines, small: Virgo

Intima: Cancer

Intoxication: Moon in Pisces

Intracranial: Aries

Introversion: Jupiter retrograde, lower hemisphere, negative signs

Invalid: Virgo

Involuntary muscle: Moon Mars Uranus

Iodine: Venus

Irregular: Uranus

Iris: Aquarius, Aries, Mars

Irritability: Mars Uranus, fire and water emphasis

Irritation: Mars

Iron in blood: Mars

Ischium: Sagittarius

Islet of Langerhans: Taurus, Virgo

Isolate: Pluto

Itching: prominent Venus receiving stress aspects from outer planets, Mars

IUD: Scorpio

J

Jaundice: Afflicted and prominent Mars and Jupiter, Saturn in Sagittarius

Jaw, lower: Taurus

Jaw, swollen: Mars afflicted in Taurus or Scorpio, afflictions in Taurus or Scorpio

Jaw, upper: Aries

Jejunum: Virgo

Joint inflammation: Mars Saturn

Joint pain: Mercury Saturn, Saturn Pluto, Mars Saturn

Joints: Cancer Capricorn axis, Mars Saturn, Nodes, tenth house

Joints, stiff: Capricorn, Sun Saturn

Jugular vein: Taurus

K

Keloid: Mars Jupiter

Ketones: Sun Jupiter

Kidney ailments: Venus Saturn, Venus Uranus, afflictions in Libra or Scorpio, Venus Mars afflictions

Kidney disease: Emphasis in cardinal signs, afflictions in Libra, Moon in Libra, Mars in Aries, Saturn in Libra stress Moon, Venus Saturn stress and involvement of sign Libra, Saturn in Libra in stress to Sun and Moon, Moon in Capricorn square Saturn in Libra, Venus square Mars, Stellium in seventh house, Planets in Virgo or Libra, Venus = Sun/Neptune, Moon = Venus/Saturn, Venus = Saturn/Neptune, Venus = Mars/Neptune, Saturn or Neptune in Libra

Kidney dysfunction: Venus Saturn, Venus Neptune

Kidney infection: Venus Mars

Kidney inflammation: Mars in Libra

Kidney, lower: Mars, Pluto, Scorpio

Kidney pain: Venus Uranus

Kidney stones: Saturn in Libra

Kidney, upper: Venus, Libra

Knee injuries: Mars in Capricorn

Knee joints: Capricorn

Knees: Capricorn

Knees, fluid: Jupiter Saturn

Knife wounds: Sun Mars affliction

L

Lacerations: Mars Uranus

Lactation: Moon, fourth house

Lacteals: Cancer

Laetrile: Neptune, Pluto

Lameness: Sagittarius, Venus Uranus, Saturn in Sagittarius

Laryngeal glands: Pisces, Cancer

Larynx: Taurus

Laryngitis: Saturn in Taurus, Mercury in Taurus, Venus Saturn

Lassitude: Moon Saturn

Lateral sclerosis: Aquarius

Lead: Saturn

Lead poisoning: Saturn in Gemini, Neptune

Leakiness: Neptune

Lecithin: Jupiter

Leg cramps: Aquarius, Sagittarius

Legs, lower: Aquarius

Legs, upper: Venus, Jupiter, Sagittarius

Lens of eyes: Mars

Leprosy: Capricorn, Saturn Neptune

Lesions: Mars Saturn

Lethargy: Mars Neptune, Venus

Leukemia: Jupiter in Pisces, Mars afflicted, Saturn or Neptune prominent

Leukocytes: Neptune

Libido: Mars

Life force: Sun

Ligaments: Saturn

Lightening: Uranus

Limbic System: Moon, Cancer

Limitation: Saturn

Limping: Saturn in Sagittarius

Linkage: Gemini, Nodes

Lipids: Jupiter

Lipoma: Mars Jupiter

Lips: Aries Taurus

Lips, lower: Taurus

Lips, upper: Aries

Liquid intake: Moon Ascendant

Liquids: Moon

Liquor: Neptune

Lisping: Mercury

Listlessness: Neptune

Liver: Sagittarius, Virgo, Jupiter

Liver action: Jupiter

Liver degeneration: Jupiter in Capricorn, Jupiter Saturn

Liver disease: Sun in Virgo afflicted by Jupiter, Jupiter in Virgo afflicted, Moon Jupiter stress aspect, Jupiter prominent and afflicted, Moon in sixth house afflicted by Jupiter, Jupiter Saturn, Jupiter Neptune, Saturn = Moon/Jupiter, Jupiter = Saturn/Neptune, Sun = Jupiter/Saturn, Jupiter = Mars/Saturn, See also Hepatitis

Liver disease, acute: Mars Jupiter

Liver, dysfunction: Mercury Mars, Mars Jupiter, Jupiter Saturn, Jupiter Uranus, Jupiter Neptune, Jupiter = Saturn/Neptune

Liver, enlarged: Jupiter in Virgo

Liver, erratic functioning: Jupiter Uranus

Liver, filtering function: Virgo

Liver, fat storage and utilization: Jupiter

Liver function: Jupiter

Liver, glycogen storage: Cancer

Liver inflammation: Mars in Virgo

Liver, lower lobes: Virgo

Liver, upper lobes: Cancer

Liver, sluggish: Jupiter Saturn, Saturn or Neptune in Sagittarius, Saturn in Pisces

Liver transplant: Pluto, Mars Pluto, Jupiter Saturn, Mars Uranus, Sagittarius emphasis, (see also Hepatitis)

Lockjaw: Taurus

Locomotive function: Gemini Sagittarius

Locomotor ataxia: Leo, Sagittarius

Locomotor disorders: Mutability, Mercury, Jupiter, third and ninth houses

Longevity: Jupiter well aspected in fourth, eighth or twelfth house or in good aspect to their rulers or planets therein, Saturn well placed in fourth house, angular and well aspected Sun, Mars or Jupiter

Loneliness: Venus Saturn

Low blood pressure: Saturn stress to Jupiter

LSD: Neptune

Lumbago: Libra emphasis, Mars in Libra, Saturn in Libra, Sagittarius

Lumbar region: Libra

Lung cancer: Mars Gemini, afflictions in mutable cross, Saturn in Gemini, Mars Jupiter

Lung disease: Saturn Neptune, afflictions in Gemini Sagittarius, Saturn or Neptune in Gemini, Pisces emphasis, afflic-

tions to Jupiter, Saturn/Neptune = Jupiter, Saturn/Neptune
= Mars

Lung hemorrhage: Jupiter

Lung inflammation: Mars in Gemini, Mercury Mars

Lungs: Gemini Sagittarius

Lyme Disease: Neptune Pluto

Lymph: Moon, Pisces

Lymphatic System: Pisces, Neptune

Lymph glands: Neptune

M

Magnesium: Sun, Jupiter, Uranus

Magnifying: Jupiter

Malaise: Sun Neptune

Malaria: prominent Mars and Neptune, Saturn or Pluto afflicted

Malformation: Pluto, Mars Saturn, Saturn Neptune

Malignancy: Saturn, Neptune, Pluto

Malnutrition: Saturn, Virgo, Lack of earth

Mammary glands: Cancer

Mammary veins: Cancer

Mania: Mercury Mars, Mercury Neptune, Neptune, Mars

Mandible: Aries

Manganese: Venus, Saturn, Pluto

Manic-depression: fire and water, Jupiter Pluto, Jupiter Uranus, Jupiter Neptune, Venus stress Mars, Venus square Saturn, Moon Saturn, Moon Uranus

Manipulative: Moon Pluto

Masked symptoms: Neptune

Mastitis: Cancer

Mastoid trouble: Moon Saturn

Masturbation: fifth house, eighth house

Maternity: Moon Venus

Measles: Mars in Capricorn, Saturn Neptune or Pluto prominent

Mechanical induction: Uranus Ascendant

Medical ability: Virgo, Scorpio, or Pisces prominent, sixth house, eighth house, twelfth house prominent

Medical discovery: eighth house

Medical profession: Mercury, Virgo, sixth house

Medicine: Saturn, Neptune, Virgo, Scorpio

Meditation: Neptune

Melancholy: Moon Venus Saturn combination, Capricorn emphasis; See also Discontent

Melanoma: Saturn in affliction, Capricorn emphasis, twelfth house emphasis

Memory: Mercury, Moon

Memory, poor: Sun/Neptune = Mercury

Meniere's Disease: Venus Saturn, Mercury in Taurus

Meninges: Cancer

Meningitis: Saturn in Sagittarius, Mercury Mars, Mars Saturn, Moon Ascendant

Menopause: Saturn Pluto, Moon

Menopause trouble: Venus affliction

Menorrhagia: Venus Mars Scorpio, Venus Pluto

Menstrual cycle: Moon, Moon Venus, Venus Pluto

Menstruation, excessive: Venus Mars, Moon Mars

Menstruation, irregularities: Moon Venus, Moon Uranus, Moon Pluto, Venus Mars, Moon in Scorpio

Menstruation, suppressed: Saturn in Scorpio

Mental aberration: Sun Uranus Neptune, Moon Saturn, Saturn Neptune, Neptune = Moon/Saturn

Mental defect: Mercury = Sun/Neptune, Mercury = Saturn/Neptune

Mental deficiency: water afflictions in third house, ruler of twelfth conjunct ruler of first

Mental disease: Uranus Neptune

Mental disorders: Mercury Uranus Neptune combination, Neptune MC, Neptune Pluto, Mercury Mars, Mercury = Neptune/MC, Neptune afflicted in third or ninth house,

Mental exhaustion: Sagittarius

Mental faculties: Mercury

Mental health worker: sixth house, twelfth house, Neptune

Mental illness: Saturn Pluto, Mercury Pluto

Mental image: Mercury

Mental instability: Moon

Mentality: third house, Mercury, Gemini

Mental strain: sixth house, Mercury Uranus, MC = Saturn/Neptune

Mental suffering: Moon Saturn, Mercury Saturn, Saturn in third house receiving stress aspects, afflictions to third house

Mercury (quicksilver): Neptune, Mercury

Metabolic malfunction: Neptune

Metabolism: solar aspects

Metabolism imbalance: Jupiter Pluto

Metabolism, weak: Jupiter Neptune, Sun Neptune

Metacarpal bones: Gemini

Metal poisoning: Saturn Pluto, Mars Saturn, Saturn Neptune

Metastases: Pluto

Metatarsus: Pisces

Microbe: Pluto

Microcytic anemia: Saturn Pluto

Micturation: Scorpio

Midget: Pluto

Migraine: Cancer, Aries, Moon and Mars combination, Saturn in Aries or Libra, Moon stress Uranus, Mercury stress Uranus, Mercury stress Mars

Mineral depletion: Saturn

Mineral deposits: Saturn

Minerals: Saturn

Miscarriage: Mars in Cancer, Malefics in fifth house or ruler of fifth afflicted, Venus stress Mars, Moon stress Saturn, Moon stress Mars, Pluto = Moon/Venus

Misdiagnosis: Neptune, Moon Neptune, Mars Neptune, Jupiter Neptune

Misinformation: Neptune

Mold: Neptune

Moles: Saturn in Capricorn

Moles on face: Saturn Ascendant, Saturn in Aries

Molybdenum: Mars

Moodiness: Water signs, Moon Pluto, Sun = Jupiter/Saturn, Uranus = Moon/MC

Moods: Sun Moon

Morbid: Saturn

Morbid fear: Mars Saturn Neptune

Morphine: Neptune

Mortification: Saturn

Mother complex: retrograde planets, Saturn in Cancer, Moon Pluto, Ascendant ruler retrograde

Motor nerves: Mercury Mars

Motor nerves in brain: Mercury MC

Mountain Fever: Leo, Mars in Leo

Mourners: Saturn Nodes

Mouth: Taurus, Aries

Mouth diseases: Aries, Taurus

Mucous: Pisces

Mucous formation: Moon

Mucous membranes: Cancer, Moon

Multiple Sclerosis: Mercury Neptune, Mercury Venus, Mercury Mars, Mercury Saturn, Jupiter Uranus, Jupiter Neptune, Saturn in Cancer or Capricorn stress to Uranus, Mars

Cancer, Mars Sagittarius, Leo Aquarius axis emphasized, Aquarius emphasis, Saturn = Uranus/Neptune, Uranus = Mercury/Neptune, Mercury = Sun/Neptune

Mumps: Mars in Taurus, Venus Mars affliction

Muscles: Mars

Muscle injury: Mars Jupiter

Muscle movement, unconscious: Moon Mars

Muscle numbness: Mars Neptune

Muscle paralysis: Mars Neptune

Muscle relaxant: Mars Neptune

Muscle spasms: Mars Uranus, Mars Ascendant

Muscle tone: Venus Mars

Muscle wasting: Mars Neptune

Muscle weakness: Mars Saturn

Muscular disorders: Mars

Muscular dystrophy: Mars Neptune, Mercury Neptune, Saturn in Capricorn

Musculoskeletal: Mars Saturn

Muscular spasm: Mars Uranus, Uranus

Muscular strain: Mars Uranus

Muscular strength: Mars

Muscular system: Fire, Mars

Muscular tension: Mars Uranus

Muscular tissue: Mars Jupiter, Sun Mars

Mutation: Pluto, Uranus Pluto

Myasthenia Gravis: Mars Neptune

Myelitis: Aquarius, Mars, Mars in Leo, Mars in Cancer

Myocardial infarction: Leo, Sun Mars Uranus

Myocarditis: Saturn in Scorpio, Mars in Leo afflicts Sun, Sun Mars Uranus combination, fifth house afflictions

Myocardium: Leo

Myopia: Afflictions to Mercury, Saturn Ascendant, Moon

Myotrophic Lateral Sclerosis (ALS) Lou Gehrig's Disease:
Mars Neptune, afflictions in Sagittarius or Aquarius, Mercury Uranus, Mutability, third or ninth house emphasis

Mysterious illness: Neptune

Myxedema: Taurus

N

Nails: Capricorn
Narcissistic: Venus
Narcotics: Neptune
Nasal bone: Scorpio
Nasal catarrh: Scorpio
Nasal discharge: Mercury Saturn, Scorpio
Nasopharynx: Taurus
Natural healing: Uranus
Naturopathy: Mercury Virgo
Nausea: Saturn in Cancer, Moon Mars, Cancer
Naval: Nodes, Cancer
Neck: Taurus
Neck abscesses: Taurus Scorpio
Necrosis: Saturn
Needle: Mars
Nephritis: Libra
Nephrosis: Saturn in Libra, Saturn in Scorpio
Nerve endings: Gemini
Nerve inflammation: Mercury Mars
Nerve irritation: Mercury Mars, Mercury Pluto
Nerve paralysis: Mercury Neptune, Mercury Uranus
Nerves, function of: Mercury Pluto

Nerves, motor: Mercury Mars

Nerve neurons: Neptune

Nerves, sensory: Mercury Venus

Nerve sheath: Moon, Cancer

Nerves, strong: Mercury Saturn

Nerves, weak: Mercury Neptune

Nervine: Mercury

Nervous agitation: Mercury Uranus

Nervous breakdown: Mercury Uranus, Uranus Pluto, Mercury Mars square Uranus, Uranus = Mercury/Neptune, Sun = Uranus/Pluto

Nervous debility: Jupiter Neptune

Nervous disorders: air and earth signs, especially Gemini and Virgo, Capricorn, and Aquarius; emphasis in third and sixth houses and planets Mercury, Saturn and Uranus, Mercury emphasized, Saturn Uranus, Moon Mercury, Sun Mercury, Moon Uranus, Sun Uranus, Mercury Jupiter, Mercury Saturn, Mercury Uranus, Venus Uranus, Mars Uranus, Saturn Uranus, Mars in Gemini, Mercury = Mars/Pluto, Mercury = Mars/Uranus. Uranus = Mercury/Pluto

Nervous irritation: Mercury Mars, Air emphasis

Nervousness: Mercury Uranus, Venus Uranus, Gemini

Nervous strain: Mercury Saturn, Mercury Mars, Mercury Pluto, Uranus Ascendant

Nervous system: Mercury, third house, Gemini, Aquarius, Uranus, Sun Uranus, Mars Uranus

Nervous system, sluggish: Mercury Saturn

Nervous temperament: Air emphasis, Uranus = Sun/Moon

Nervous tremor: Gemini

Nervous twitches: Uranus

Neuralgia: Mercury Mars, Uranus Ascendant, Gemini

Neurasthenia: Mercury Uranus afflictions, Mercury Saturn afflictions

Neurons: Mercury Neptune

Neurosis: Moon Saturn, Mercury emphasized, Mercury Neptune

Neurotic: Venus Neptune, Mercury Neptune

Neuritis: Mars in Sagittarius, Mercury stress aspect to Mars or Uranus, 29o Gemini Sagittarius

Neurotransmitters: Uranus

Niacin: Venus, Mercury

Nicotine: Pluto, Neptune

Nipples: Cancer

Nitroglycerin: Uranus Neptune

Nodules: Taurus

Non-malignant: Venus

Nose: Aries

Nosebleeds: Aries, Mars in Taurus or Scorpio

Nourishment: Moon

Nuclear medicine: Pluto

Nucleus: Sun

Numbness: Mercury Saturn, Sun Neptune

Nursing home: Saturn Nodes

Nutrient absorption: Moon

Nutrients: Jupiter

Nutrition: Sun Pluto, Cancer, sixth house

Nutritionist: Mercury in sixth house, Cancer Virgo emphasis, Neptune

Nurturance: Moon

O

Obesity: emphasis in Taurus Cancer Sagittarius, Sun Jupiter, Venus Jupiter in Cancer, Moon Jupiter, Jupiter Ascendant, water emphasis, stellium in second house or in Taurus

Obsession: Pisces, Pluto

Obstetrics: Moon, Cancer

Obstinacy: Moon Saturn

Obstruction: Saturn

Occipitals: Aries

Occlusion: Saturn

Ointment: Venus Saturn

Old age: fourth house

Olfactory nerve: Venus

Oncologist: Mars Pluto

Operation: Mars

Ophthalmology: Moon, Mercury, Aries

Opiates: Jupiter Neptune

Opium: Neptune

Optic nerve: Mercury Aries

Optician: Moon, Mercury, Aries, Neptune

Optimism: Jupiter or Sagittarius emphasis, Sun and Mars, Leo and Aries emphasis

Oral candidiasis: Taurus, Neptune, Venus Neptune

Oral fixation: fourth house

Orchitis: Scorpio

Organ Atrophy: Mars Saturn

Organ donor: seventh house

Organ, enlarged: Jupiter

Organ lesions: Mars

Organ regeneration: Jupiter Pluto favorable aspects

Organ removal: Saturn Uranus

Organs: Sun

Organs of storage: Moon

Organ, underdeveloped: Saturn Pluto

Organ weakness in the body: Saturn/Neptune, sign placement of Saturn or Neptune

Ossicles: Aries

Ossification: Saturn

Osteoarthritis: Capricorn

Osteomalacia: Saturn Neptune

Osteomyelitis: Prominent Mars and Saturn afflicted, Pluto

Osteopathy: Saturn in Capricorn, Mercury in Virgo

Osteoporosis: Saturn Neptune

Otolaryngologist: Taurus, Aries, Mercury Mars

Ovarian complaints: afflictions in Venus or Cancer, Moon Venus

Ovarian cyst: Moon Pluto

Ovarian disease: Sun or Moon in Scorpio afflicted, Venus in Taurus or Scorpio, Pluto to the Sun or Moon, fourth house emphasis, afflictions to eighth house

Ovaries: Cancer or Scorpio, Venus Pluto, Moon

Ovary, left: Moon

Ovary, right: Sun

Ovary trouble: Venus afflictions, Moon square Mars in Cancer

Overactivity: Uranus

Overdose: Neptune

Overexertion: Mars Uranus
Overindulgence: Jupiter
Ovulation: Moon, Venus Pluto
Ovulatory pain: Moon Uranus
Oxidation, high: Mars in Aquarius
Oxidation, poor: Saturn in Aquarius
Oxygen: Sun, Aquarius, Saturn Aquarius, Mars Aquarius
Oxygenation: Gemini, Aquarius
Oxygenation of blood: Gemini, Sun, Aquarius

P

PABA: Sun, Saturn

Pacemaker: Pluto, Uranus

Paget's Disease: Capricorn

Panthothenic acid: Neptune

Pain: Mars

Palate: Taurus

Pallor: Moon Saturn

Palpitation: Leo

Palsy: Mercury or Moon afflicted by Uranus or Neptune, Jupiter Saturn stress, Mercury Neptune

Pancreas: Virgo

Pancreas, diseases of: Mercury Jupiter

Pancreatis: Mars in Virgo

Pangamic acid: Jupiter, Uranus

Panic: Uranus

Pantothenic acid: Mars Neptune

Paralysis: Uranus, Sun Saturn, Prominent and afflicted Uranus, Mars Neptune, Uranus Neptune, MC = Sun/Saturn

Paralysis, spastic: Mercury Mars

Paralyzed muscles: Mars Saturn

Paranoia: Mercury Pluto, Pisces, Neptune

Parasites: Venus Virgo afflicted, Moon conjunct Venus in Virgo, Mercury afflicted in Virgo, Moon afflicted in Cancer or Virgo, Pluto prominent, Mars Pluto

Parathyroid glands: Aquarius, Saturn

Parkinson's Disease: Gemini Sagittarius, Aquarius, Uranus aspecting Sun or Moon, Mars Uranus, Mercury Uranus, Saturn Uranus

Paroxysms: Aquarius

Passivity: Moon, Jupiter Neptune

Patella: Capricorn

Pathology: Pluto, Scorpio

Pediatrician: Moon Mercury

Pellagra: Saturn afflicted

Pelvis: Scorpio

Pelvic operation: Mars in Sagittarius

Penis: Pluto, Scorpio, Mars

Pepsin: Cancer

Peptic ulcer: Cancer

Perfectionist: Virgo

Pericarditis: Mars in Leo, Cancer and Leo connection, Virgo

Pericardium: Cancer

Periodicity: Moon

Periodontist: Mars Saturn, Taurus

Peristalsis of bowels: Virgo

Peristalsis of intestines: Jupiter Uranus

Peristalsis of stomach: Cancer

Peristaltic action: Virgo

Peritoneum: Cancer

Peritonitis: afflictions to Moon or Cancer, afflicted planets in Virgo or to Mercury, Mars in Virgo, Sun, Moon, Mars in Virgo receiving hard aspects from Saturn, Uranus, Neptune or Pluto

Permeability: Neptune

Perspiration: Moon

Perversity: Uranus

Pessimism: Virgo, Saturn, Mercury Saturn, Mutability, Saturn Neptune, Saturn = Sun/Mercury

Phalanges: Gemini, Pisces, Capricorn

Phallus: Pluto

Pharmacologist: Scorpio, Neptune, Mars

Pharyngitis: Taurus

Pharynx: Taurus

Phlebitis: Venus Mars in stress aspect, Venus Aquarius, Venus prominent and heavily afflicted, Uranus affecting fixed planets

Phlegm: Pisces

Phobia: Saturn Neptune, Neptune in third house, Neptune influencing sixth or eighth houses, water signs, Gemini or third house emphasis

Phosphorus: Mars, Saturn

Physical body: Ascendant

Physical change: Pluto Ascendant

Physical degeneration: Sun Pluto

Physical development, slow: Sun/Pluto = Saturn

Physical discomfort: sixth house

Physical disorders: Sun

Physical examination: sixth house

Physical exhaustion: Mars, Sagittarius

Physical handicap: Sun Saturn

Pigmentation: Saturn in Libra, Venus Saturn, Capricorn

Piles: Scorpio, Saturn Pluto

Pimples: Mars in Capricorn, Aries

Pimples on face: Sun

Pineal gland: Pisces, Neptune

Pituitary: Aries, Cancer Capricorn, Venus MC

Pituitary deficiency: Moon afflicted

Pituitary gland, interior: Sun

Pituitary gland, posterior: Jupiter

Pituitary overproduction: Mars Pluto

Placenta: Cancer, Scorpio

Plague, sickness from: Sun/Neptune = Saturn

Plaque: Cancer Capricorn, Neptune

Plasma: Moon

Plasma balance: Libra

Plastic: Neptune

Pleasure sensations: Venus

Plethora: Sun, Jupiter or Venus in affliction

Pleura: Cancer

Pleurisy: Cancer, Mars, Neptune, Saturn Gemini, Mercury Mars stress aspect, Jupiter Saturn, Neptune in Gemini or Cancer

Pneumonia: Saturn in Gemini, Mars in Sagittarius, Mercury Pluto, Moon Pluto, Sun Pluto and involvement of sign Gemini, afflictions in Gemini Sagittarius, combination of Saturn, Mercury and third house, Moon stress Saturn, Mars Saturn Neptune combination, Mercury Pluto

PMS: Moon Venus, Moon Mars, Moon Ascendant, Moon Uranus

Pneumogastric nerve: Mercury

Podiatry: Jupiter, Neptune, Pisces

Poison: Neptune

Poison accumulation: Saturn Pluto

Poisoning: Mars Neptune, Saturn Neptune

Poison, noxious: Pluto

Poliomyelitis: Sun Mars Neptune, Saturn prominent, Sun Uranus, Mercury Uranus, Mercury Pluto, Uranus afflictions with Leo or Aquarius, Neptune = Sun/Pluto, Pluto = Sun/Neptune, MC = Sun/Saturn

Polyps: Taurus, Mars in Taurus

Pons Varolii: Sun, Aries

Portal: Virgo

Possession: Neptune

Posterior pituitary gland: Cancer, Sagittarius, Jupiter

Potassium: Moon

Potency, low: Neptune = Moon/Mars

Prana: Sun

Pregnancy: Cancer, Moon Jupiter, Moon Venus, Moon Pluto

Pregnancy, False: Neptune Pluto

Preservatives: Neptune

Preventative medicine: sixth house, Mercury

Probe: Pluto

Procrastination: Neptune Pluto

Procreative function: Taurus Scorpio

Prostate, enlarged: Mars in Taurus

Prostatectomy: Mars in Scorpio, Mars Uranus

Prostate disease: Mars Pluto, Mars Uranus, eighth house emphasis, Scorpio

Prostate gland: Scorpio

Prostate trouble: Mars Pluto, Scorpio afflictions

Protectiveness: Cancer

Prostheses: Neptune

Protozoa: Pluto

Pruritis: Mars in Scorpio

Psoriasis: Mars in Capricorn, Venus Neptune afflictions

Psychiatric treatment: twelfth house, sixth house

Psychiatrists: eleventh house, sixth house, Uranus

Psychic disorders: Neptune

Psychical disease: Moon Saturn

Psychic healing: Neptune

Psychoanalysis: eighth house, Pluto
Psychologist: eighth house, Jupiter, Pluto, Uranus
Psychological problems: Moon
Psychosis: Neptune
Psychosomatic illnesses: Moon Neptune, Pisces
Psychotic: Neptune
Ptomaine poisoning: Saturn Neptune
Puberty: Sun Pluto, Venus Mars
Puberty of a woman: Moon Mercury
Pubic bone: Scorpio
Public health: sixth house
Pulmonary artery: Leo
Pulmonary circulation: Gemini
Pulmonary disease: Mercury Saturn, Saturn in Gemini, Sun =
    Jupiter/Saturn
Pulmonary disorders: Gemini
Pulmonary emphysema: Venus Saturn
Pulp of teeth: Taurus
Pulse: Sun Uranus
Punctures: Mars
Pupil (eyes): Sun Moon, Aries
Purging: Pluto
Putrification: Pluto
Pus: Mars Neptune, Pluto
Pyelitis: Libra, Scorpio
Pyloric trouble: Virgo, Mercury
Pyorrhea: Saturn in Taurus, Neptune
Pyridoxine: Moon, Mercury, Mars

Q

Quack doctor: Neptune
Quarantine: Saturn
Quinine: Neptune
Quinsy: Taurus

R

Radiation: Sun
Radiation, atomic: Uranus
Radiologist: Uranus, Aquarius, Sun
Radionics: Uranus
Radius: Gemini
Rape: Venus = Mars Pluto
Rare illness: Aquarius
Rashes: Mars in Aquarius, Mars Uranus
Reactivity: Mars
Receptive: Moon
Rectum: Scorpio
Recurring illness: Mutability
Red blood cells: Mars
Redness: Mars
Reflex action: Mercury Mars, Moon
Reflex channels: Mercury Jupiter
Regeneration: Pluto, Sun Jupiter, Jupiter Pluto
Regression: Pluto
Regulative function: Aries Libra
Rejuvenation: eighth house, Pluto
Relapse: Venus
Relaxing: Venus, Neptune, fifth house

Remission: Uranus

Renal calculi: Libra

Renal colic: Libra, Mars in Libra

Renal function: Aries Libra

Renal irritation: Venus Mars

Renal retention: Saturn in Aries or Libra

Renal system: Venus, Libra, sevenh house and its ruler

Replication: Pluto

Reproductive activity: Pluto, Scorpio

Reproductive organs, diseases of: Scorpio, Venus Saturn, Moon Pluto

Reproductive urge: Venus Mars

Resistance: Sun Jupiter

Resistance, lowered: Sun Saturn afflictions

Respiration: third house, Mercury, Gemini

Respiratory allergies: mutability, prominent Moon or Neptune, Cancer, Mercury, Gemini, Sagittarius, see also Allergies

Respiratory disorders: Moon Mercury, Mercury, Gemini, mutability, third house emphasis, Saturn in third house, Moon Saturn

Respiratory system: Mercury, Gemini Sagittarius, Afflictions to third and ninth houses and their rulers

Restlessness: Gemini, Uranus, Sun Mars

Restricted activity: Mars Saturn

Retardation: Saturn, Sun/Mercury = Saturn

Retarded development: Sun/Saturn = Pluto

Retention: Saturn

Retention of metabolic waste: Saturn Neptune

Retina: Aquarius, Mercury Mars, Sun,

Rheumatic ailments: Saturn afflictions and involvement of Mars, Mars Saturn stress aspect, Mars Saturn, Saturn Uranus

Rheumatic fever: Mars in Leo, Mars in Sagittarius, Mars Saturn

Rheumatism: Saturn, Sun Saturn, Sagittarius

Rheumatism in arms, hands or shoulders: Saturn in Gemini

Rheumatoid arthritis: Saturn Neptune with Mars Saturn, Saturn in twelfth house, Neptune in tenth house

Rhinitis: Mars in Taurus, Mar Jupiter afflictions, Mars in Cancer, Mars in Scorpio

Rib cage: Cancer

Riboflavin: Mars, Moon

Rickets: Saturn, Capricorn

Rigidity: Saturn

Rigor: Sun Saturn

Rigor mortis: Saturn

Ringworm: Venus Mars afflictions

Rips: Mars

RNA: Pluto

Rupture: Mars Saturn, Jupiter Saturn, Scorpio, Uranus, Virgo afflictions

Rutin: Venus

S

Sacral Region: Scorpio

Sacroiliac: Sagittarius

Sacrum: Scorpio

Sadism: Pluto

Saliva: Moon Neptune

Salivary glands: Taurus, Neptune, Cancer

Salts: Saturn

Saphenous vein: Sagittarius

Sarcoma: Saturn Pluto

Scabies: Venus Mars afflictions

Scalds: Mars, Sun Mars

Scales: Saturn

Scalp: Aries

Scar: Mars Uranus

Scar tissue: Mars Uranus, Saturn

Scarlet Fever: Mars in Leo

Schizophrenia: Sun Neptune, Moon Pluto, Sun Uranus, Mercury Gemini stress to Neptune, Moon Uranus, Moon Pluto, Saturn Neptune, Mars Uranus, Venus Saturn, afflictions involving Aries or first house, Mercury Pluto, Uranus = Neptune/MC

Sciatica: Mars in Sagittarius or Gemini afflicted, Saturn in Sagittarius

Sciatic nerve: Sagittarius, ninth house
Sclerosis: Capricorn
Sclerosis of the liver: Saturn in Virgo
Scrapes: Mars
Scrofula: Saturn Pisces, Taurus
Scrotum: Scorpio
Scurvy: Cancer Capricorn
Sebaceous: Jupiter
Seclusion: Saturn Ascendant
Secretions: Moon
Sedative: Neptune
Sedentary: Venus
Seizures: Uranus, Moon Mars, Saturn Uranus, Ascendant =
    Jupiter/Uranus
Selenium: Mars, Jupiter, Pluto
Selfishness: Mars, Saturn
Self-indulgence: Jupiter
Self-poisoning: Saturn Pluto
Semen: Cancer, Scorpio
Senility: Saturn
Sensation: Libra, Gemini
Senses: Mercury, Taurus, Venus
Sensitive body: Sun Neptune, See also Body
Sensitivity to allergens: Moon Ascendant, see also Allergies
Sensory nerves: Mercury Venus
Sensuality: Venus
Sepsis: Saturn Neptune
Septic: Saturn
Septicemia: Mars Neptune
Septic inflammation: Sagittarius
Septic poisoning: Mars in Scorpio

Serous: Moon

Serous membranes: Moon, Cancer

Serum: Sun Moon

Sex: Mars

Sex organs, female: Pluto, Scorpio, eighth house, Venus

Sex organs, male: Pluto, Scorpio, eighth house, Mars

Sexual diseases: Venus Pluto

Sexual dysfunction: Mars, Pluto

Sexual intercourse: fifth house, Pluto, Scorpio, Venus Mars

Sexuality: Venus Mars

Shank: Aquarius

Shingles: Mars in Leo, Mars Uranus emphasis and involvement of signs Cancer, Leo, or Virgo, Moon Mercury

Shins: Aquarius

Shock: Uranus

Shoulders: Gemini, Mercury

Shrinking: Neptune, Saturn

Sickness: sixth house, Virgo, Mercury

Sick room: sixth house, twelfth house

Side of body: fifth house, Sun, Leo

Sight: Gemini, Mercury, Sun Moon, see also Eyes

Sight, defective: afflictions to Gemini, Aquarius or Capricorn Ascendant, Sun Moon in hard aspect

Sight, unequal: Sun and Moon in affliction to each other

Sigmoid Flexure: Scorpio

Silica: Sagittarius

Silver: Moon

Sinews: Mars

Sinus cavity: Cancer

Sinus trouble: Jupiter Saturn Aries Scorpio

Sinusitis: Cancer, Gemini, Mars

Skeletal system: Earth, Saturn, Cancer Capricorn

Skin: Capricorn, Saturn, Venus, Libra

Skin ailments: Venus Mars, Saturn Ascendant, Venus Ascendant

Skin allergies: prominent Moon or Neptune, Venus Saturn, Saturn in Cancer or Capricorn, Mars in Capricorn, Venus Mars or Venus Pluto stress, afflictions in Aries Libra, see also Allergies

Skin cancer: Saturn in Capricorn

Skin, cosmetically: Libra

Skin crawling: Nodes Ascendant

Skin disease: Saturn Capricorn, Venus Saturn, Venus Mars, Mars in Capricorn, Moon Saturn, Saturn Pluto

Skin disorders: Venus Saturn

Skin, dry: Saturn in Capricorn, Venus Saturn

Skin eruptions: Libra

Skin grafting: Saturn Pluto

Skin growths: Pluto, Venus Pluto

Skin injuries: Mars Saturn

Skin rash: Libra

Skin sensitivity: Uranus Ascendant, Aquarius

Skin swelling: Venus Mars

Skull: Saturn

Sleep: Pisces

Sleep disorders: Neptune

Sleeping sickness: Neptune

Sluggishness: Moon Venus

Smallpox: Mars in Capricorn, Venus Mars, Mars, Aries, Venus

Smell, sense of: Mercury, Jupiter, Mars, Scorpio

Sneeze reflexes: Taurus

Social diseases: Uranus Nodes

Sodium: Moon

Sodium chloride: Aquarius, Saturn

Sodium hydrate: Mars
Sodium phosphate: Libra, Venus, Saturn
Softening: Neptune
Somnambulism: Neptune, twelfth house
Soporific: Neptune
Sores: Mars
Sorrow: Saturn
Spasmodic: Uranus
Spasm: Uranus, Mercury Uranus, Mars Uranus, Jupiter Uranus, Uranus Pluto
Spasmodic: Aquarius
Spastic colon: Sun Uranus, Mars Uranus, Mars in Scorpio, see also Colon
Spastic disorders: Jupiter Uranus
Spastic paralysis: Mercury Mars
Speech: Mercury
Speech defects: Uranus, Gemini, Mercury
Speech organs: Mercury Saturn
Sperm: Sun Mars
Spina Bifida: Saturn in Leo, Sun Saturn
Spinal cord: Leo, Sun
Spinal curvature: afflictions in fixed signs, Leo Aquarius, Sun Saturn, Mare in Leo, Saturn in Aquarius
Spinal fluid: Neptune, Leo
Spinal meningitis: Leo, Sun afflicted
Spinal problems: Mars Uranus, Uranus Neptune
Spine: Leo, Sun
Spine, dorsal region: Sun, Leo
Spine, lumbar region: Libra
Spleen: Pisces
Spleen, inactive: Saturn in Pisces
Spleen trouble: Sun Saturn afflictions

Spondylolisthesis: Leo Aquarius, Saturn in Leo or Aquarius, Saturn Pluto

Sprain: Mars

Sprained ankle: Mars in Aquarius

Sprained finger: Mars in Gemini

Sputum: Cancer, Scorpio

Squinting: Mercury stress to Mars or Uranus

Stagnation: Saturn Neptune, fixity, water and earth

Stammer: Mercury in third house or twelfth house afflicted, Mercury Uranus, emphasis in Gemini or Virgo or third house, Mercury afflicted by Mars and Saturn, mutable afflictions

Starch: Venus

Starvation: Moon Saturn, afflictions in fourth or tenth houses, Saturn in Cancer

Stenosis: Saturn

Sterility: Saturn in Libra, Saturn in Scorpio

Sternum: Cancer Capricorn

Stiff neck: Taurus

Stiffness: Mercury Saturn

Stillborn: Uranus Neptune, Moon Pluto, Pluto = Moon/Venus

Stimulant abuse: Neptune

Stimulation: Mars

Stomach: Cancer

Stomach acid: Mars in Cancer

Stomach allergies: cardinal emphasis, Cancer rising or on sixth house cusp, Moon Mars, Moon Neptune, Moon afflicted

Stomach cramps: Cancer Capricorn, Uranus in Cancer

Stomach disorders: afflictions in Cancer Capricorn, Moon afflicted, Mars or Saturn in Cancer, cardinality, fourth house emphasis

Stomach, low acid: Saturn in Cancer

Stomach upset: Mars in Cancer

Stones: Sun or Moon afflicted by Saturn or by Uranus in a Saturn sign

Strain: Gemini

Strangulation: Taurus

Strangury: Mars in Scorpio, Saturn in Scorpio

Strep and staph mixture: Mars Neptune

Stress: Moon Uranus, Mars Uranus, Uranus Pluto, Uranus

Strictures: Uranus

Stroke: malefics rising or close to the Ascendant, Moon Aries, Saturn stress to Ascendant, Mars Aries, Jupiter afflicted in Taurus, Leo, Scorpio or Aquarius, Mars in Aries in sixth house, Sun in Aries with Mars afflicted, Jupiter or Sun in Aries and afflicted

Structural function: Cancer Capricorn

Structural weakness: Saturn Neptune

Stubbornness: Taurus

Stunting: Neptune

Stupor: Neptune

Stutter: see Stammer

St. Vitus's Dance: Sun Uranus, Mercury Uranus

Styptic: Saturn

Subconscious mind: Moon Mercury, Nodes

Sucrose: Venus

Submissiveness: Moon

Sudden death: Uranus

Sudden illness: Mars, Uranus = Sun/Neptune

Sudorific: Sun Moon

Suffering: Saturn Neptune

Suffocation: Mars Saturn, Saturn in Taurus

Sugar: Venus

Sugar addiction: Venus, Libra, Taurus and Pisces

Sugar metabolism: Venus Pluto, Taurus

Sugar metabolism failure of: Jupiter Uranus, Venus/Pluto = Saturn

Suicidal tendencies: Afflictions to eighth house

Suicide: Uranus, Mars afflictions, twelfth house emphasis, ruler of twelfth afflicted, Saturn stress aspect to Sun, Moon or Ascendant

Sulfur: Saturn

Sunburn: Aries

Sunstroke: Sun, Leo, Mars square Ascendant, Sun opposite Moon, afflictions in Aries, Mars in Libra, Mars in Leo

Superiority: Sun, Mars, Jupiter

Support: Taurus

Surgeon: eighth house, Pluto MC , Mars/Uranus = Mercury

Surgery: Mars Uranus, Mars Nodes, Mars Ascendant, Mars/Uranus = Sun, Mars/Uranus = Mercury

Surgery, female: Mars/Uranus = Moon, Moon/Uranus = Moon

Surgical cutting: Mars Uranus

Surgical operations: Mars, Mars Ascendant

Surgical removal: Mars/Jupiter = Saturn

Sweat: Sun Moon

Sweaty feet: Mars in Pisces

Sweaty hands: Aries, Libra, Scorpio, Moon

Swelling: Sun Jupiter, Jupiter, Sun Pluto

Swelling of hands or feet: Jupiter in Gemini, Jupiter in Pisces, Libra

Swollen glands: Taurus

Swooning: Leo

Sympathetic nervous system: Mercury, Uranus

Syncope: Leo, Neptune Pluto

Synopses: Mercury, Saturn

Synthetic drugs: Neptune

Synovia: Pisces

Synovial fluid: Moon, Pisces

Synovitis: Capricorn

Syphilis: Gemini Sagittarius, Venus Mars afflicted, Mars opposite Uranus and involvement of Taurus or Scorpio

Systemic Lupus Erythematosus: Aries Libra, Cardinality, Mars in Libra, Sun Neptune, Pisces or twelfth house, Mars Neptune, Mars is Pisces, Venus Saturn

T

Tachycardia: Leo, prominent Uranus, Uranus in sixth house
Tactile stimulation: Venus
Tapeworm: Virgo
Tarsus: Aquarius
Tartar: Saturn in Aries
Taste: Venus
Tears: Moon, Neptune
Teeth: Capricorn
Teeth, bad: Saturn, Sun Saturn, Mars Saturn
Teeth, false: sixth house. Neptune
Teeth grinding: Saturn in Aries
Temper: Mars
Temples: Jupiter
Tenacity: Cancer
Tendon: Nodes, Gemini, Mars, Saturn
Tension: Mars, Mercury, Moon Uranus, Sun Uranus
Testes: Scorpio
Testicles: Scorpio
Tetanus: Uranus
Thiamine: Mercury
Therapy: Pluto MC
Thighs: Sagittarius

Thigh injury: Mars in Sagittarius

Thinking capacity: Moon Mercury

Thirst: Mercury Mars

Thoracic duct: Cancer

Thorax: Cancer

Thoughts: Mercury

Throat: Taurus

Throat cancer: Taurus, Saturn in Taurus

Throat problems: Saturn in Taurus or Scorpio

Throat, sore: Taurus

Thrombophlebitis: Venus Mars

Thrombosis: Venus Jupiter, Venus Pluto and prominent Saturn or Neptune

Thrombus: Saturn

Thumbs: Taurus, Aries

Thymus gland: Taurus, Neptune

Thyroid gland: Taurus

Thyroid complications: Sun Mercury, Mercury Pluto, Mars in Taurus, Pluto = Moon/Mercury

Thyroid imbalance: Sun = Moon/Mercury

Tibia: Aquarius

Tick Fever: Mars Neptune

Tics (spastic): Mercury Mars, Mars Uranus, Uranus Ascendant

Timidity: Saturn

Tin: Jupiter, Neptune

Tissue inflammation: Sun Mars

Tissue relaxation: Venus

Tissues, soft: Venus Jupiter

Tissues, waterlogged: Jupiter Neptune

Tobacco: Mars Neptune

Toes: Pisces

Tone, lack of: Neptune Nodes

Tongue: Gemini, Taurus, Mercury

Tongue, sensory receptors: Taurus

Tonic: Mars, Sun

Tonsils: Taurus

Tonsils, removal or infection: Taurus on sixth or eighth house cusp, Taurus or Scorpio rising, Mars or Saturn in Taurus or Scorpio, Venus in stress aspect with Saturn, Neptune or Pluto

Toothache: Aries, Saturn in Libra, Saturn in Aquarius

Tooth decay: Saturn in Aries, Saturn in Taurus

Tooth trouble: Prominent Saturn

Torpid: Neptune

Touch: Venus

Tourette Syndrome: Pluto, Mercury Uranus, Mercury Mars, Mars Uranus

Toxemia: Sun Pluto, Mars Neptune, Pluto, Scorpio

Toxic conditions: Neptune Pluto, Mars Neptune, Moon Neptune, Pluto = Mars/Neptune

Toxic fumes: Saturn/Neptune = Ascendant or MC

Toxic substance: Neptune, Pluto

Trachea: Gemini, Taurus

Trance: Neptune

Transference: Gemini Sagittarius

Transplant: Mars Pluto

Trauma: Mars

Tremors: Mars Uranus

Trench mouth: Mars Saturn, Mars in Taurus

Trigeminal neuralgia: Uranus Ascendant, Aries, Mercury Mars, Mercury Uranus

Tubal pregnancy: afflictions in Gemini, Saturn, Mars or Pluto in stress aspect to Venus or the Moon

Tuberculosis: Neptune in mutable sign aspect Sun or Moon, mutable emphasis, Saturn in Gemini or Sagittarius or Pisces, Saturn Neptune

Tubes: Gemini

Tumor, benign: Moon with Jupiter, Saturn or Neptune

Tumor formation: Neptune = Sun/Saturn, Moon = Saturn/ Neptune

Tumors: Taurus, Sun Neptune, Sun Pluto, Moon Jupiter, Venus Jupiter, Jupiter Neptune, Saturn Uranus Neptune combination, Sun or Moon with Neptune, Sun or Moon with Saturn, Jupiter = Sun/Saturn, Neptune = Sun/Moon

Twisted: Uranus

Twitching: Mercury Mars, Mercury Uranus, Uranus

Tympanic: Taurus Cancer

Typhoid: Saturn Scorpio, Mars in Virgo

Tyranny: Scorpio

U

Ulceration on legs or thighs: Mars in Sagittarius
Ulcerative: Mars
Ulcers: Mars in Cancer, Uranus Ascendant, Cancer, Virgo
Unconscious: twelfth house, Neptune, Moon
Underactivity: Saturn
Underdeveloped organ: Saturn
Undernourishment: Moon Saturn
Underweight: Mercury
Undulant Fever: Moon Mars
Unease: Neptune
Unusual: Uranus
Uranium: Uranus
Urination, painful: Venus Mars
Urea: Saturn
Uremia: Libra
Ureter: Gemini
Urethra: Scorpio
Urethral stricture: Scorpio
Uric acid: Jupiter
Uric acid deposits: Saturn
Urinary calci: Venus Saturn
Urinary disorders: Mars in Scorpio

Urinary tract: Libra, Aries, Scorpio

Urine: Scorpio, Pluto, Moon

Urine, suppression: Moon Saturn

Urogenital system: Scorpio

Uterine tumor: Venus afflicted, afflictions in Scorpio or Mars afflicted

Uterus: Cancer

Uterus, tipped: Saturn in Scorpio

Uterus trouble: Scorpio, Venus Mars afflictions and Moon afflicted

Uvula: Taurus

V

Vaccines: Neptune

Vagus nerve: Mercury

Vagina: Scorpio

Vaginitis: Mars in Scorpio

Valve: Aquarius

Vanadium: Jupiter, Saturn

Varicose veins: Venus afflicted, Moon, Venus or Jupiter in Aquarius, Saturn in Aquarius or Gemini, afflictions to Leo or Aquarius, Venus square Uranus, Venus Mars, Moon Venus or Jupiter in Aquarius, Saturn = Sun/Neptune, Uranus afflicted, Venus Jupiter Saturn in hard aspect, Venus Jupiter or Venus Neptune combination, Venus in Aquarius stress Saturn, Venus Saturn, Mars in Aquarius

Varicosities: Venus Aquarius conjunct Saturn, Venus Saturn

Vas deferens: Gemini

Vasomotor system: Aquarius

Vasopressor: Mars Saturn

Vegetarianism: Virgo, Mercury in Aquarius aspecting Uranus, prominent Neptune, Sun Neptune

Veins: Venus

Veins, inflammation: Venus stress Mars, Venus in Aries

Veins, loss of elasticity: Venus Saturn

Vena cava: Leo

Venereal disease: Mars in Scorpio, Moon in Scorpio, Uranus Neptune, Venus stress Mars

Venereal disease, susceptibility: Sun/Neptune = Mars, Venus stress Mars, eighth house

Venereal ulcers: Mars in Scorpio

Venous blood circulation: Venus

Ventral hernia: Mars in Virgo, Mars in Pisces

Vermin, disease from: Pluto Ascendant

Vertigo: Aries, Moon Mercury and Saturn

Vesicant: Mars

Victim: Neptune Pisces

Violent insanity: Uranus = Mercury/Mars

Virility, high: Sun Mars, Sun Pluto

Virility, low: Mars Neptune

Virus: Neptune, Pluto

Virus infection: Pisces, Pluto Ascendant

Viscera: Moon

Viscosity: Moon

Vital fluid: Sun

Vitality: Sun, Sun Moon, Sun Mars, Mars Jupiter

Vitality, lowered: Sun Saturn, Moon Saturn, Sun in hard aspect to Moon, Saturn in sixth house, Sun = Saturn/Neptune

Vitamins: Sun

Vitamin A: Sun

Vitamin B1: Mercury

Vitamin B2: Mars, Moon

Vitamin B3: Venus, Mercury

Vitamin B5: Mars Neptune

Vitamin B6: Moon, Mercury, Mars

Vitamin B12: Mars

Vitamin B15: Jupiter, Uranus

Vitamin B17: Pluto

Vitamin C: Saturn
Vitamin D: Sun
Vitamin E: Venus
Vitamin F: Jupiter
Vitamin K: Saturn, Jupiter
Vitamin P: Saturn, Venus
Vivifying: Leo
Vocal chords: Taurus
Voice: second house, Taurus
Volition: Mercury
Vomiting: Cancer
Vulva: Scorpio

W

Waist: Libra

Warts: Venus Pluto, Capricorn

Wasting: Saturn Neptune

Water: Moon

Water imbalance: Moon Saturn, Moon Neptune, Sun Moon

Water retention: Moon, Water sign on Ascendant

Weak body defenses: Sun Neptune, See also Body

Weather sensitivity: Uranus Nodes, Aquarius

Weight gain: Jupiter, Sun Pluto

Weight loss: Saturn, Sun Pluto

Weight problems: Sun Jupiter, Jupiter in sixth house, Sagittarius rising, water emphasis, Moon in Taurus or Cancer

Weird ailments: Pisces

Wheezing: Saturn in Gemini

Whiplash: Mars in Taurus

White blood cells: Neptune

Whooping Cough: Mercury or Gemini planets afflicted, Saturn, Neptune, Pluto prominent, Saturn in Taurus

Willfulness: Uranus

Will to live: Sun

Windpipe: Gemini, Taurus

Withdrawal: Neptune

Withering: Saturn Neptune

Womb: Cancer, Moon Venus

Workaholic: Venus in Capricorn

Worms: Mars in Virgo

Worry: Mercury Saturn, Mercury Neptune, Mercury Ascendant, Saturn Neptune, Neptune in twelfth house

Wounds: Mars Aries, Mars

Wrinkles: Saturn

Wrist: Gemini

Wrist joints: Cancer

Writer's cramp: Mars Uranus

X

X-rays: Uranus

Y

Yeast: Pisces

Yellow Fever: Mars afflicted and prominent in affliction with Saturn, Neptune or Pluto

Youth: Moon Mercury

Youthfulness: Gemini and Sagittarius, Venus Saturn

Z

Zinc: Mars, Jupiter, Venus

Uranian Astrology

Brief Description of the
Uranian Planets in Medical Astrology

Cupido: sugar balance, birth, illness in the family

Hades: deterioration, wasting, breaking down, decay, withering

Zeus: procreation, conception, sperm, burns, gunshot wounds

Kronos: medical expert, physical height

Apollon: complications, spreading, epidemics, multiply

Admetos: suffocation, blood clots, choking, finality, a cast, a specialist

Vulcanus: recuperation, physical prowess

Poseidon: cosmic protection

* * *

Abortion: Neptune = Mars/Zeus, Mars + Zeus - Hades

Accidents: Uranus Hades

Acute Disease: Sun = Hades/Zeus

AIDS: Ascendant + Hades – Mars

Amnesia: Aries Neptune

Appetite, poor: Venus Hades

Artificial insemination: Pluto Zeus

Birth, premature: Saturn + Hades - Venus

Bladder sickness: Saturn + Hades = Venus

Blood disease: Mars = Sun/Hades, Aries + Neptune - Sun

Blood disorders: Neptune = Sun/Hades; Sun + Hades – Mars = Neptune

117

Bodily power: Sun Vulcanus

Body, misshapen: Sun/Hades = Moon

Breast disease: Moon Hades

Cancer: Aries + Hades − Neptune = Sun, Saturn + Neptune − Hades, Saturn + Hades − Neptune

Blood poisoning: Aries + Neptune

Blood pressure: Sun Zeus

Body sensitivity: Kronus = Sun/Neptune

Bone ailments: Saturn Hades

Cast: Admetos

Chemicals: Neptune + Hades - Apollon

Choking: Admetos

Circulation: Aries Admetos

Creativity: Moon Zeus

Cruelty: Hades

Danger: Uranus Hades

Death: Pluto Admetos

Death, unusual: Uranus Admetos

Death, mysterious: Neptune Admetos

Debility: Sun + Sun - Saturn

Deformities: Sun Hades

Depression: Aries + Admetos = Mercury, Pluto/Hades = Mercury

Diet, special: Admetos = Sun/Pluto

Disease, chronic: Sun + Hades - Saturn

Disease, rare: Uranus Hades

Disintegration: Hades

Dropsy: Neptune Hades

Drowning: Neptune + Hades

Dwarfism: Sun Admetos

Emotional strength: Moon Vulcanus

Epidemic: Aries + Hades, Aries + Saturn = Hades
Epidemic, susceptible to: Sun/Neptune = Hades
Family illness: Cupido Hades
Feet problems: Neptune Hades
Female ailments: Moon Hades
Fever and sepsis (blood poisoning): Vulcanus
Feverish: Sun Zeus
Food, tainted: Sun/Hades = Pluto
Gangrene: Hades
Gas poisoning: Moon + Vulcanus - Neptune
Geriatric diseases: Saturn + Nodes - Uranus = Hades
Glandular disorder: Sun + Moon - Jupiter = Hades
Gluttony: Apollon = Sun/Pluto
Graveyard: Ascendant + Admetos
Growths, deep: Pluto Admetos
Gunshot: Zeus
Handicapped: Sun/Saturn = Admetos
Healthy offspring: Moon Zeus
Hereditary weakness: Sun/Neptune = Zeus
Hidden illness: Hades
Hindrance: Admetos
Hunger: Hades = Sun/Pluto
Hysterectomy: Mars + Hades - Saturn
Immobility: Mars Admetos
Infection of the blood: Aries + Neptune – Hades
Illegitimate birth: Pluto Hades
Illness, lingering: Saturn Hades, Neptune Hades
Illness, end: Neptune Admetos, Hades Admetos
Illness, fated: Neptune Vulcanus
Illness, fighting: Hades Zeus
Illness, lingering: Saturn Hades

Illness, short: Uranus Hades
Immobility: Mars Admetos, Saturn Hades
Inertia: Admetos
Lightning strike: Zeus
Liver action: = Jupiter
Liver complaints: Aries + Hades = Jupiter
Liver disease: Jupiter Hades
Lung action: Sun + Hades = Jupiter
Medicare: Kronos
Melancholy: Saturn Hades
Mental power: Mercury Vulcanus
Migraine headaches: Vulcanus
Miscarriage: Uranus Zeus, Sun + Zeus - Hades
Misery: Hades
Muscular strength: Mars Vulcanus
Mutilated body: Sun Hades, Sun/Hades = Vulcanus
Narcotic addition: Sun/Neptune = Hades
Numbness in limbs: MC + Neptune - Mercury
Nutrition, poor: Hades = Sun/Pluto
Obsessive-compulsive behavior: Zeus
Pain: Hades, Mars Hades
Pain, lingering: Jupiter Hades
Paralysis: Hades Vulcanus, Hades + Vulcanus = MC
Physical endurance: Sun Admetos
Physical troubles: Sun Hades
Physician: Sun/Hades = Ascendant
Plague: Aries Hades
Poison, deadly: Neptune Admetos
Polio: Zeus + Hades – Mercury
Post Traumatic Syndrome: Zeus
Pregnancy: Moon Zeus, Aries + Pluto

Pregnancy, difficult: Saturn Zeus
Pregnancy, pleasant: Pluto Cupido
Pregnancy, termination: Pluto Admetos
Procreative function: Mars Zeus, Moon, Zeus, Zeus Nodes
Puberty: Zeus = Sun/Pluto
Quarantine: Aries + Saturn = Neptune
Radiating pain: Mars Apollon
Radiation: Admetos + Admetos - Poseidon
Rupture: Uranus Admetos
Sanitariums: Venus + Neptune - Kronos
Sexual perversion: Hades Zeus
Sexual suppression: Mars Admetos
Shock: Uranus Admetos
Sick mother: Pluto Hades
Sick woman: Moon Hades
Skin disease: Sun/Hades = Venus
Sperm: Venus Zeus
Sterility: Neptune Zeus, Neptune = Venus/Zeus
Sterility, voluntary: Venus Hades
Stomach trouble: Moon Hades
Stoppage: Admetos
Stroke: Uranus Admetos
Stunted growth: Pluto Hades
Suffocation: Admetos
Surgeon: Mars Kronos
Susceptibility: Aries + Neptune
Toxic illness: Pluto Hades
Traction: Admetos
Tropical fever: Aries + Hades - Juiter
Tuberculosis: Saturn + Hades - Jupiter, Neptune + Hades - Jupiter

Twins: Apollon
Vermin, disease from: Hades
Viral infection: Neptune + Mars - Apollon
Vitality: Sun Vulcanus
Vitality, lack: Poseidon = Sun/Hades
Weakness: Neptune Vulcanus
Weight gain: Sun/Pluto = Admetos
Will, the: Uranus Zeus
Withering: Hades
Woman, strong: Aries + Vulcanus = Moon
Womb disease: Aries + Moon – Saturn, Moon + Hades
Worry: Moon Hades
Wound, open: Mars Admetos

Bibliography

Bertucelli, Penelope. *Phoenix Workshop Uranian Astrology Manual Cosmobiology Conference*. Penelope Publications, Plantation, FL, 1995.

Berkow, Robert, M.D., Beers, Mark, M.D., Fletcher, Andrew, M.D. *The Merck Manual of Medical Information Home Edition*. Merck Research Laboratories, Whitehouse Station, NJ, 1997.

Bills, Rex E. *The Rulership Book*. Macoy Publishing & Masonic Supply Co., Inc., Richmond, VA, 1976.

Brau, Jean-Louis, Weaver, Helen and Edmands, Allan. *Larousse Encyclopedia of Astrology*. New American Library, NY and Scarborough, ON, 1977.

Carter, C.E.O. *An Encyclopaedia of Psychological Astrology*. The Theosophical Publishing House Ltd., London, 1963.

Cornell, H.L. *Encyclopaedia of Medical Astrology*. Samuel Weiser, Inc., York Beach, ME, 1972.

Cramer, Diane. *How To Give An Astrological Health Reading*. AFA, Tempe, AZ, 1996.

Daath, Heinrich. *Medical Astrology*. Health Research, Moke-lumne Hill, CA, 1963.

Darling, Harry F. *Essentials of Medical Astrology*. AFA, Tempe AZ, 1981.

Davidson, William. *Davidson's Medical Astrology*. Astrological Bureau, Monroe, NY. 1979.

Davison, R.C. *The Technique of Prediction*. L.N. Fowler & Co. Ltd., London, 1972.

Doane, Doris Chase. *Astrology: 30 Years Research*. AFA, Tempe AZ, 1979.

Ebertin, Reinhold. *Astrological Healing: The History and Practice of Astromedicine*. Samuel Weiser, Inc., York Beach ME, 1989.

Ebertin, Reinhold. *The Combination of Stellar Influences*. Ebertin-Verlag, Aalen, Germany, 1972.

Gibson, Mitchell E., M.D. *Signs of Mental Illness*. Llewellyn Publications, St. Paul, MN, 1998.

Harmon, J. Merrill. *Complete Astro-Medical Index*. Astro- Analytics Publications, Van Nuys, CA, 1979.

Harvey, Ronald. *Mind & Body in Astrology*. L.N. Fowler & Co., Ltd., Essex, England, 1983.

Heindel, Max and Heindel, Augusta Foss. *Astro-Diagnosis: A Guide To Healing*. The Rosicrucian Fellowship, Oceanside, CA, 1973.

Jansky, Robert Carl. *Astrology Nutrition & Health*. Para Research, Rockport, MA, 1977.

Jansky, Robert C. *Essays in Medical Astrology*. Astro-Analytics Publications, Van Nuys, CA, 1980.

Jansky, Robert Carl. *Introduction to Holistic Medical Astrology*. AFA, Tempe, AZ, 1983.

Jansky, Robert C. *Modern Medical Astrology*. Astro-Analytics Publications, Van Nuys, CA, 1978.

Lewis, Anthony. *Horary Astrology the History and Practice of Astro-Divination*. Llewellyn Publications, St. Paul, MN, 1991.

Lilly, William. *Christian Astrology, Books I and II*. Ascella Publications, London, 1999.

Mann, A.T. *Astrology and the Art of Healing*. Unwin Paperbacks, London, 1989.

Mayo, Jeff. *The Planets and Human Behaviour*. The Camelot Press, Ltd., London, 1973.

Millard, Margaret. *Casenotes of a Medical Astrologer*. Samuel Weiser, Inc., NY, 1950.

Mindell, Earl *Vitamin Bible*. Warner Books, NY, 1979.

Munkasey, Michael. *Midpoints Unleashing the Power of the Planets*. ACS Publications, San Diego, CA, 1991.

Nauman, Eileen. *The American Book of Nutrition & Medical Astrology*. Astro Computing Services, San Diego, CA, 1982.

Niemann, Henry & Cooper, Judith. *Astrology of Psychology*. AFA, Tempe, AZ, 1936.

Ridder-Patrick, Jane. *A Handbook of Medical Astrology*. Arkana, London, 1990.

Rothenberg, Robert E. *Medical Dictionary and Health Manual*. New American Library, Inc., NY, 1982.

Rudhyar, Dane. *An Astrological Study of Psychological Complexes*. Shambhala Publications, Inc., Berkeley, CA, 1966.

Rudolph, Ludwig, (Witte-Verlag). *Rules for Planetary Pictures*. Hamburg, Germany. 1974.

Sellar, Wanda. *Introduction to Medical Astrology*. The Wessex Astrologer, Bournemouth, England, 2008.

Smith, Samuel. *Atlas of Human Anatomy* (Revised). Text by Barnes & Noble Books, NY, 1961.

Starck, Marcia. *Astrology Key to Holistic Health*. Seek-It Publications, Birmingham, MI, 1982.

Starck, Marcia. *Medical Astrology Healing for the 21st Century*. Earth Medicine Books, Santa Fe, NM, 2002.

About the Author

Diane L. Cramer, a resident of New York City, began studying astrology in 1973. At the same time she began studying health and nutrition. In the 1980s she began an intensive study of medical astrology, culminating in the publication of her first book *How to Give an Astrological Health Reading*, first published by the AFA in 1988 with a revised edition published in 1996. The revised edition of *Dictionary of Medical Astrology* utilizes her vast experience and study of medical astrology to give the reader a user-friendly compilation of terms and significators used in medical astrology. She has since published *Managing Your Health and Wellness* (Llewellyn) and *Medical Astrology: Let the Stars Guide You to Good Health* (Jove Press).

Diane is a teacher, lecturer and counselor in all aspects of astrology. She specializes in writing and instructing on medical astrology and nutrition. She is a member of the education faculty of the NCGR in New York City and has published articles on medical astrology in the *NCGR Journal*, *Today's Astrologer* (AFA), and Dell *Horoscope*, as well as the *Uranian Journal* of the Uranian Sig.

Professional affiliations include: American Federation of Astrologers (AFA), National Council for Geocosmic Research (NCGR), and the Uranian Society.

Diane has masters and post-masters degrees in education from Hunter College in New York City and a B.A. in English, speech and journalism from the University of Florida. She has also passed the highest certification of the NCGR and holds a CA NCGR Level IV.

www.ingramcontent.com/pod-product-compliance
Lightning Source LLC
Chambersburg PA
CBHW032103080426
42733CB00006B/397